The … Series

LEEDS UNITED

Seasons 1983-84 to 1992-93

Season-by-Season Commentary
Don Warters

Statistics and History
Mike Ross

Editors
Michael Robinson, John Robinson & Philip Norminton

CONTENTS

British Library Cataloguing in Publication Data
A catalogue record for this book is available from the British Library
ISBN 0-947808-31-0

Printed by Adlard Print & Typesetting Services, The Old School, The Green, Ruddington, Notts. NG11 6HH

LEEDS UNITED FIRSTS by Mike Ross

Although Leeds United did not come into being until 1919, it is important to go back a number of years to trace the club's true origins. As early as 1880, Hunslet AFC played at Holbeck, Leeds on the rugby club ground and in 1896 they helped to found the West Riding County FA. Such was the club's prominence that it won the County Challenge Cup in four successive seasons from 1897 to 1900 and in 1904, Leeds City was formed to expand upon Hunslet's lead. Within a year, no doubt assisted by the Football League's determination to challenge Rugby's West Riding supremacy, the club was elected to Division Two and at the end of the 1905-06 season, were well-placed in sixth position. In the seasons that followed, Leeds City achieved no great success but were, nevertheless, a good middle-of-the-road club despite having to seek re-election at the end of the 1911-1912 season.

Leeds City FC
pictured before the formation of Leeds United

League Football recommenced in 1919, but City soon found themselves in trouble with the Football Association as a result of allegations that illegal payments had been made to players during the war years (when a local syndicate had rallied around to save the club from extinction after it had fallen into the hands of the receiver). Despite demands from the FA, the club failed to produce their books of account for inspection and Leeds City found themselves in the unenviable position of becoming the first and, so far, only, League club to be wound up by the parent body. So thorough was the League's action that all the players were put up for auction and club's fixtures taken over by Port Vale, who were elected in City's place.

Within a very short time, Leeds United was formed out of the ashes of Leeds City when it was made known that support would be forthcoming from both the FA and Football League.

Meanwhile, the neighbouring town, Huddersfield was also in dangers of losing its club (through lack of support) and a proposal was made to transfer the club to Leeds. Although the move was never made, Mr. Hilton Crowther (who had backed Huddersfield during the lean years of World War One) decided to switch his allegiance to the newly-formed club and, with his powerful support, Leeds United were elected into the Second Division of the Football League for the 1920-21 season. (There can be little doubt that this extraordinary move was connived at by the numerous member clubs of the Football League, who had evaded disciplinary action for similar offences when Leeds City was made a scapegoat).

Ironically, Leeds United travelled to Port Vale (the team that had taken over the fixtures of Leeds City the season before) for their first game which they lost 2-0. A week later they gained their revenge over Port Vale with a 3-1 victory over Port Vale at Elland Road and, at the end of the season, were comfortable settled midway up the table. Three seasons later, Leeds achieved their first honour when they won the Second Division Championship.

Leeds United's first spell in the top flight was far from successful and they struggled to avoid relegation for two seasons before dropping down at the end of the 1926-27 season. They finished 1927-28 as Second Division runners-up and struck much better First Division form when they returned in 1928-29.

After finishing fifth in 1929-30, Leeds were relegated in 1930-31 but, once more, won their way back up the following season. They retained their First Division status throughout the 1930's but, after World War Two, had a really awful 1946-47 season when they finished bottom, seven points behind the next placed club, Brentford, and 15 points behind third-from-bottom Huddersfield.

Leeds soon established themselves as a top-notch Second Division outfit, but it was not until the end of the 1955-56 season that they regained First Division status. In 1960, Leeds found themselves back in the Second Division but after they had fought their way back to the top flight by winning the Second Division Championship in 1963-64, under the guidance of Don Revie, they entered their most successful period ever. In 1964-65 they won the same number of points as Manchester United, but had to be content with runners-up position on goal-average and finished runners-up again the following season.

After two seasons in fourth place, Leeds at last won the First Division Championship in 1968-69 and then had to be content with second and third place over the next three seasons, before winning the Championship again in 1973-74.

In Europe, Leeds enjoyed success too, appearing in two consecutive Fairs Cup Finals, losing the first to Dinamo Zagreb but winning the second against Ferencváros in 1968. Leeds also reached the 1973 Cup-Winner's Cup Final and the 1975 European Cup Final, losing both and acquiring, in the process, a reputation as Europe's 'bad-boys' when their ill-disciplined fans caused havoc on the terraces.

At the end of the 1981-82 season, Leeds were relegated to the Second Division having finished in 20th position.

CLUB FIRSTS

First Recorded Game
15th November 1919 vs Yorkshire Amateurs (friendly) - score 5-2

First Competitive Game
22nd November 1919 vs Barnsley (Midland League) - score 0-0

First F.A. Cup Game
11th Sept 1920 vs Boothtown (h) - score 5-2

First F.A. Cup Scorer
Len Armitage

First F.A. Cup Draw
13th January 1923 vs Portsmouth (a) - score 0-0

First F.A. Cup Defeat
7th January 1922 vs Swindon Town (a) - score 1-2

First F.A. Cup Semi-Final
27th March 1965 vs Manchester United (at Hillsborough) - score 0-0

First F.A. Cup Final
1st May 1965 vs Liverpool (at Wembley) - score 1-2

First F.A. Cup Final Scorer
Billy Bremner

First F.A. Cup Final Victory
6th May 1972 vs Arsenal (at Wembley) - score 1-0

First Football League Match
28th August vs Port Vale (a) - score 0-2

First Football League Scorer
Len Armitage (vs South Shields, 1st Sep 1920)

First Football League Draw
11th Sep 1920 vs Leicester City (a) - score 1-1

First League Championship Win
1968-69

First Championship of any Division
1923-24, Second Division

First League Cup Tie
28th September 1960 vs Blackpool (h) - score 0-0

First League Cup Win
5th October 1960 vs Blackpool (a) - score 3-1

First League Cup Defeat
5th Dec 1960 vs Southampton (a) - score 4-5

First League Cup Scorer
Don Revie

First League Cup Semi-Final
17th Jan 1968 vs Derby County (a) - score 1-0

First League Cup Final
2nd Mar 1968 vs Arsenal (Wembley) - score 1-0

Leeds United, 2nd Division Champions 1923-24

LEEDS UNITED SEASON 1983-84

Failure to win back First Division status at the first attempt had sentenced Leeds United to another term in Division Two, but hopes were high at the outset that the Elland Road club would make it back to the top flight in this season.

Player-manager Eddie Gray, who had begun a clear-out of players the previous season, had brought much-needed new blood into the club, signing Aberdeen midfielder Andy Watson and striker George McCluskey from Celtic at a cost of £200,000. However, he also had to try to balance the books and transferred defender Paul Hart to Nottingham Forest, winger Arthur Graham to Manchester United and John Lukic, to Arsenal, for fees totalling £180,000.

It soon became apparent that United were not promotion material but more suited to mid-table surroundings and they actually dropped as low as 19th in early January before rallying to finish in a still disappointing 12th place.

There had been little joy for United in the FA Cup as they were knocked out in the third round by Fourth Division Scunthorpe United after being bundled out of the League Cup by Oxford United.

The final game of the season, at home to Charlton Athletic, marked the end of Gray's playing career which had spanned 22 years during which time he made 579 league and cup appearances with United.

LEEDS UNITED SEASON 1984-85

Peter Lorimer, only a few months short of his 38th birthday, had been given a one-year contract with Leeds United for the start of the season, having re-joined the club on a monthly basis in the second half of the previous season.

The player who had earned the nickname 'Hot-shot' because of the ferocious power he packed in his right foot, played in midfield but still managed to overtake the club's aggregate goal scoring record of 153, which had been held by the legendary Welshman John Charles.

Eddie Gray had bought young central defender Andy Linighan from Hartlepool for a modest outlay of £15,000 and home grown talent such as Denis Irwin, Neil Aspin, John Sheridan, Scott Sellars, Martin Dickinson and Tommy Wright were making their mark in senior grade soccer.

Four successive league wins got United off to a great start, the diminutive Wright scoring five goals in those four games but they lost ground and spent most of the season hovering around sixth place. Mid-way through the campaign, Gray invested £35,000 in Aston Villa's former West Ham and Orient goalkeeper Mervyn Day and bought burly striker Ian Baird from Southampton for £50,000.

Day managed to keep nine clean sheets in 18 games and Baird scored six goals in seven appearances, but United had to be content with finishing in seventh place.

LEEDS UNITED SEASON 1985-86

Leeds United were installed as the bookmakers' favourites to win the Second Division championship but Elland Road followers, having become used to seeing such faith being misguided, were sceptical and took nothing for granted.

As it turned out, they were right, for the season quickly developed into a troubled one for United - and one of great sadness, as it marked the end of Eddie Gray's 22-year association with the club.

An opening day defeat to Fulham, and home draws against Wimbledon and Hull City were followed by a 6-2 humiliation at Stoke and when United lost their next game, at home to Charlton, they slumped to 20th place in the Second Division.

The alarm bells were sounding and dissatisfaction was expressed in the board room. United had climbed back to 11th place by the time they cane up against Third Division Walsall in the League Cup and being held to a goalless draw at Elland Road did little to appease Gray's critics.

His days as manager were numbered and even though Walsall were beaten 3-0 in the second leg of the cup tie, it was too late. The axe fell and the board's choice of successor went to another former Elland Road 'old boy' - Billy Bremner.

There was no immediate improvement. United went out of the League Cup to Aston Villa, lost to Peterborough in the FA Cup and finished 14th in the Second Division.

LEEDS UNITED SEASON 1986-87

Billy Bremner had led Leeds United through the best years of their existence as a battling midfield player and in his first full season in managerial charge went very close to bringing further glory to the club.

He moved out a number of players, including Any Linighan and martin Dickinson and pulled off a good signing when he paid Aston Villa £65,000 for defender Brendan Ormsby, who went on to play a key role in United's best season since they were relegated in 1981-82.

Victories over Telford, Swindon, Queen's Park Rangers and Wigan took them into the Semi-final of the FA Cup where they met First Division Coventry City in what turned out to be a thrilling clash.

United took a shock lead through David Rennie, but Coventry pulled back and went 2-1 up before seasoned striker Keith Edwards, coming on as a substitute, grabbed a late equaliser only for United to end up losing 3-2 in extra time.

There was more disappointment for United when, having reached the promotion play-off final. they took Charlton to a final replay at Birmingham and after leading 1-0 with seven minutes left, the First Division was beckoning, but they then conceded two late goals.

Nineteen goals from Ian Baird, 16 from John Sheridan, nine by Keith Edwards and half a dozen from Ormsby had graced United's campaign and taken them so very close to honours.

LEEDS UNITED SEASON 1987-88

An extended contract was Billy Bremner's reward for having taken the club to within a whisker of League and FA Cup glory the previous season but United failed to live up to expectations.

Brendan Ormsby, who has suffered a severe knee injury in the promotion play-off final replay, was missing for the season, but Glynn Snodin, from Sheffield Wednesday, Gary Williams, from Aston Villa, and Bobby Davison from Derby County were recruited as another bid for promotion took place.

Many had believed this season would see the re-awakening of United, who were often described as a slumbering giant among soccer clubs, but it was not to be. The progress made in the last season was not continued, though the campaign did see David Batty, a precocious young player whom Bremner predicted a bright future for, make his league debut.

The Leeds born Batty, a battling midfielder, in many ways similar to Bremner himself, made his appearance in a 4-2 home victory over Swindon Town - a game in which £350,000 striker Bobby Davison marked his debut for Leeds by scoring one of the goals.

United spent the last third of the season camped just outside the top six of the Second Division and finished in 7th place while Oldham Athletic had ended their League Cup hopes and Aston Villa had proved too good for United in an FA Cup third round tie.

LEEDS UNITED SEASON 1988-89

Billy Bremner became the seventh manager to "vacate" to Elland Road hot-seat in the 14 years after Don Revie left to manage England.

The axe fell on Bremner in late September after United had won just once in their first six League games and this time the board changed their recent policy by not going for a former Elland Road player. Their choice was Howard Wilkinson.

United were languishing perilously close to the foot of the Second Division when Wilkinson left his managerial job with Sheffield Wednesday to begin his "rescue" act and his first job was to tighten up the defensive part of his new side.

His first three games in charge produced draws, two of them away from home, before Hull City's visit to Elland Road produced his first win. Although United went out of the League Cup to Luton Town, their League progress continued and a run of ten successive league games without defeat took them into 14th place.

United became a difficult team to beat and climbed as high as sixth in the table before having to settle for a final placing of tenth.

Just before the March transfer deadline, however, Wilkinson pulled off a master stroke when he persuaded Scottish international Gordon Strachan to sign in a £300,000 deal. Times were about to change for the better for United . . .

LEEDS UNITED SEASON 1989-90

Having bought Gordon Strachan and Chris Fairclough towards the end of the previous season for a total outlay of £800,000, Howard Wilkinson continued to show that United really meant business by splashing out close to £2m for John Hendrie, Mel Sterland and Vinny Jones.

Promotion to the First Division was a serious aim this term and understandably they were hot favourites to go up. But Wilkinson's expensive side took a shock 5-2 tumble at Newcastle on the opening day of the season and suffered further setbacks in following games.

After five matches, United were down in 12th position but a narrow away win over Hull City proved to be a turning point and the surge was on. They rose to second place by mid October but had to wait until December to take over top spot from Sheffield United.

Although the Blades kept up a strong challenge, United were in a position they were never to surrender. They suffered a setback when they lost narrowly at Watford and were then held to a goalless draw at home to Port Vale in March but it proved to be little more than a hiccup on the way to glory.

Promotion was deservedly clinched and the Second Division Championship followed, although United needed a last day victory at Bournemouth to be certain of lifting the trophy, and this duly came, courtesy of a lone goal from Lee Chapman.

Leeds United F.C., 1989-90 season

Howard Wilkinson and his team celebrate after winning the 2nd Division Championship

LEEDS UNITED SEASON 1990-91

A crowd of 34,500 settled in at Goodison Park as United played their first match back in the First Division since 1981-82 and on the face of it, Everton presented tough opposition for Howard Wilkinson's newly-promoted side.

But United quickly showed they could be more than a match for the soccer elite of the country. Chris Fairclough scored the first goal back in the big time, Gary Speed added a second and when Imre Varadi got one on the hour, United were coasting to victory. Goals from Pat Nevin and John Ebbrell put the pressure on but United held on.

Arsenal needed four attempts to knock United out of the FA Cup, at the fourth round stage, and Howard Wilkinson's men reached the semi-finals of the League Cup before losing to Manchester United and were knocked out of the Zenith Data Systems Cup by Everton in the northern area final.

United had certainly acquired a 'taste' for life at the top and went through the league campaign so well that they finished in fourth position, Lee Chapman showing the way with a 31 goal tally - 21 of them in the league.

But Gordon Strachan's experience and his influential play proved to be invaluable as United became a force again in English soccer while youngsters David Batty and Gary Speed took to top division competition remarkably comfortably. As they say . . . United were back!

LEEDS UNITED SEASON 1991-92

Confidence is high and expectations are great whenever a new season kicks off but in a realistic sense, Leeds United felt that to do better than the last season, when they finished fourth, would be quite an achievement.

Just as he had done each close season since taking over the managerial reins at Elland Road, manager Howard Wilkinson had spent heavily in the transfer market.

English international left-back Tony Dorigo had checked in from Chelsea, speedy young forward Rod Wallace from Southampton, and Steve Hodge arrived from Nottingham Forest for a combined outlay of close to £4m.

A goal from Gary McAllister got United off to a winning start against Nottingham Forest but only a late equaliser from Hodge earned them a draw at home to Sheffield Wednesday in their next game.

By mid-September, United were in second place and a ding-dong championship battle with Manchester United began in earnest. The two Uniteds were never out of the top two for the rest of the season, first one and then the other enjoying the glory of heading the First Division.

The Old Trafford Side knocked Leeds out of the League Cup at the quarter-final stage and beat them in the third round of the FA Cup but Wilkinson's men had the last laugh when pipped their Manchester rivals for the League Championship in the penultimate game of the season.

Leeds United F.C. - League Champions 1991-92

Howard Wilkinson and his players celebrate after the Championship triumph

LEEDS UNITED SEASON 1992-93

Howard Wilkinson's men, as League Champions were the team everyone wanted to beat when the new Premier League was launched. Sadly, for the thousands of United supporters, it was to prove a season of unfulfilled expectations.

Although they kept another first class home record losing only once, to Nottingham Forest, they suffered the embarrassment of being unable to win a single away game in the Premier League.

They became the only top division champions not to do so and there was little consolation for them in the cup competitions, Watford knocking them out of the Coca-Cola Cup and Arsenal ending their active interest in the F.A. Cup.

United desperately wanted to do well in the European Cup, which gave them a first round two-leg tie against German Champions VfB Stuttgart, who opened up a 3-0 lead in the first leg.

The odds were piled high against them, but United turned in an unforgettable display at Elland Road, goals from Gary Speed, Eric Cantona, Lee Chapman and a penalty from Gary McAllister earning them a 4-1 second leg success to leave the score at 4-4 on aggregate.

The Germans were through on the away goals rule . . . or so we thought. But Stuttgart had fielded more than the permitted number of 'foreign' players and UEFA ordered a third game to be played, in Barcelona, which United won 2-1.

United's joy was shortlived. They fell to Glasgow Rangers in the second round and United's season went downhill after that.

1983-84

1	Aug	27	(h)	Newcastle U	L	0-1		30,806
2		29	(h)	Brighton & HA	W	3-2	Watson, Gray F., Sheridan	13,303
3	Sep	3	(a)	Middlesbrough	D	2-2	Gray F. (pen), McCluskey	12,793
4		6	(a)	Grimsby T	L	0-2		7,000
5		10	(h)	Cardiff C	W	1-0	McCluskey	12,336
6		17	(a)	Fulham	L	1-2	Ritchie	10,055
7		24	(h)	Manchester C	L	1-2	Ritchie	21,918
8	Oct	1	(a)	Shrewsbury T	L	1-5	Ritchie	6,289
9		8	(a)	Sheffield W	L	1-3	Gray F. (pen)	26,814
10		14	(h)	Cambridge U	W	3-1	Hird, Watson, Donnelly	9,923
11		22	(a)	Barnsley	W	2-0	Donnelly, Barnes	18,236
12		29	(h)	Portsmouth	W	2-1	Watson, Barnes	16,254
13	Nov	5	(h)	Crystal Palace	D	1-1	McCluskey	12,847
14		12	(a)	Blackburn R	D	1-1	Donnelly	9,556
15		19	(a)	Derby Co	D	1-1	Ritchie	16,726
16		26	(h)	Chelsea	D	1-1	McCluskey	20,680
17	Dec	3	(a)	Carlisle U	L	0-1		6,845
18		15	(a)	Charlton A	L	0-2		6,285
19		26	(h)	Huddersfield T	L	1-2	Wright	23,791
20		27	(a)	Oldham A	L	2-3	Wright, Gray F.	23,497
21		31	(h)	Middlesbrough	W	4-1	Sellars, Wright, McCluskey 2	14,129
22	Jan	2	(a)	Manchester C	D	1-1	Bond (og)	34,441
23		21	(h)	Fulham	W	1-0	Watson	11,421
24	Feb	4	(h)	Shrewsbury T	W	3-0	Watson 2, Brown A.	10,628
25		11	(a)	Cardiff C	W	1-0	McCluskey	9,407
26		15	(h)	Swansea C	W	1-0	Lorimer	10,031
27		18	(a)	Portsmouth	W	3-2	Wright, Watson, Lorimer	13,911
28		25	(h)	Barnsley	L	1-2	Wright	19,138
29	Mar	3	(a)	Crystal Palace	D	0-0		8,077
30		10	(h)	Blackburn R	W	1-0	Butterworth	12,857
31		17	(h)	Grimsby T	W	2-1	Aspin, Sellars	14,412
32		24	(a)	Brighton & HA	L	0-3		12,605
33		28	(a)	Newcastle U	L	0-1		30,877
34		31	(h)	Sheffield W	D	1-1	Ritchie	25,343
35	Apr	7	(a)	Cambridge U	D	2-2	Barnes, Sellars	4,700
36		14	(h)	Derby Co	D	0-0		12,549
37		21	(a)	Huddersfield T	D	2-2	Wright, Barnes	16,270
38		24	(h)	Oldham A	W	2-0	Ritchie, Lorimer (pen)	9,576
39		28	(a)	Chelsea	L	0-5		33,447
40	May	5	(h)	Carlisle U	W	3-0	Gavin, Ritchie, McCluskey	8,278
41		7	(a)	Swansea C	D	2-2	Wright, Lorimer	5,498
42		12	(h)	Charlton A	W	1-0	Wright	13,254

FINAL LEAGUE POSITION: 13th in Division Two

Appearances

Sub Appearances

Goals

Harvey	Thomas	Gray F.	Sheridan	Brown	Dickinson	Watson	McCluskey	Ritchie	Donnelly	Barnes	Butterworth	Hamson	Aspin	Gavin	Hughes	Gray E.	Burns	Wright	Hird	McGoldrick	Sellars	Lorimer	Irwin	Thompson	
1	2	3	4	5	6	7*	8	9	10	11	12														1
1	2	3	4	5	6	7	8	9		11	12	10*													2
1	10	3	7	5	6	4	8	9	12	11*			2												3
1	10	3	7	5	6	4	8		12		11		2*9												4
	2	3	10*	5	6	4	8	9			12			11	1	7									5
	2	3	10	5	6	4	8	9			12			11	1	7*									6
1	2	3	7	5	6		8*	9	10					11			4	12							7
1	2	3	7	5*	6	12	8	9	10					11			4								8
1	11	3	7		6	4*	8	9	10	12							5		2						9
1	11	3	7		6	4	8	9	10								5		2						10
1	11	3	7*		6	4	8	9	10	12							5		2						11
1	7	3		6		4	8	9	10	11			2				5								12
1	7	3			6	4*	8	9	10	11	12		2				5								13
1		3			6	4	8	9	10	11			2				5	7							14
1	7	3			6	4	8	9	10	11							5			2					15
1	7	3			6	4	8	9	10	11							5			2					16
1	7*	3		6	2	4	8	9	10	11		12					5								17
1		3			6	4*	8	9	10	11		12					5	7		2					18
1		3			6		8	9	10*			4					5	7	12	2	11				19
1		3			6		8*	9	10			4	5					7	12	2	11				20
1		3			6		8	9	10*			4	5					7		2	11	12			21
1		3			6		8*	9	10			4	5					7		2	11	12			22
1						4		9		11		3	5					7	2		8	10	6		23
1				5	6	4	12	9		11		3						7	2		8*	10			24
1				5	6	4	12	9		11*		3						7	2		8	10			25
1				5	6	4	12	9		11*		3						7	2		8	10			26
1				5	6	4	12	9		11		3						7	2		8	10			27
1		6		5		4	9*			11		3		12				7	2		8	10			28
1	12			5		4				11				9		3*		7	2		8	10	6		29
1					6	4*		9		11	12	3	5					7	2		8	10			30
1				5	6			9		11		3	4					7	2		8	10			31
1		3*		5	6			9		11	12		4					7	2		8	10			32
1					6			9		11	7	3	5						2		8	10	4		33
1					6			9		11	7	3	5						2		8	10	4		34
1				6				9		11	7	3	5					12	2*		8	10	4		35
1					6			9	4*	11		3	5	12				7			8	10	2		36
1					6	4	12	9	10*	11		3	5					7				8	2		37
1					6	4		9	8			3	5	11				7				10	2		38
1					6	4	12	9				3	5	11				7			8*	10	2		39
1				6		4	12	9	8			3	5	11				7				10	2		40
1				6		4	12	9*	8			3		11				7				10	2	5	41
1				6		4	9		8			3	5					7				10	2		42
40	16	24	11	22	34	30	24	38	23	25	4	23	21	10	2	4	13	23	16	7	19	20	12	1	
	1					1	8		2	2	7	2		2				2	2			2			
		4	1	1		7	8	7	3	4	1		1	1				8	1		3	4			

1984-85

1	Aug	25	(a)	Notts Co	W	2-1	Wright 2	12,196
2		27	(h)	Fulham	W	2-0	McCluskey, Wright	14,207
3	Sep	1	(h)	Wolverhampton W	W	3-2	Lorimer, Wright 2	17,843
4		8	(a)	Grimsby T	W	2-0	Lorimer, McCluskey	13,290
5		12	(a)	Cardiff C	L	1-2	Sellars	7,500
6		15	(h)	Portsmouth	L	0-1		19,438
7		22	(a)	Crystal Palace	L	1-3	Sellars	9,460
8		29	(h)	Oldham A	W	6-0	Linighan, Ritchie 3, Sheridan, Wright	14,290
9	Oct	6	(h)	Sheffield U	D	1-1	Lorimer (pen)	25,547
10		13	(a)	Barnsley	L	0-1		16,199
11		20	(a)	Huddersfield T	L	0-1		15,257
12		27	(h)	Middlesbrough	W	2-0	Lorimer (pen), Ritchie	14,838
13	Nov	3	(a)	Charlton A	W	3-2	Gavin, McCluskey, Sheridan	6,950
14		10	(h)	Carlisle U	D	1-1	Dickinson	13,327
15		17	(h)	Brighton & HA	W	1-0	Ritchie	13,127
16		24	(a)	Oxford U	L	2-5	Lorimer, Wright	12,192
17	Dec	1	(h)	Wimbledon	W	5-2	Ritchie 3, Sellars, Wright	10,899
18		8	(a)	Shrewsbury T	W	3-2	Linigham, Ritchie 2	6,358
19		15	(h)	Birmingham C	L	0-1		15,854
20		22	(a)	Wolverhampton W	W	2-0	Gray, McCluskey	9,259
21		26	(a)	Blackburn R	L	1-2	McCluskey	20,149
22		29	(h)	Cardiff C	D	1-1	Lorimer (pen)	11,798
23	Jan	1	(h)	Manchester C	D	1-1	Ritchie	22,626
24		19	(h)	Notts Co	W	5-0	Irwin, Sheridan, Wright 3	11,369
25	Feb	2	(a)	Oldham A	D	1-1	Lorimer (pen)	8,824
26		9	(h)	Grimsby T	D	0-0		12,517
27		23	(h)	Charlton A	W	1-0	Lorimer	10,664
28		26	(a)	Carlisle U	D	2-2	Aspin, Wright	5,484
29	Mar	2	(a)	Middlesbrough	D	0-0		8,781
30		9	(h)	Huddersfield T	D	0-0		18,607
31		12	(a)	Portsmouth	L	1-3	Sheridan	16,208
32		16	(h)	Barnsley	W	2-0	Lorimer, Sellars	13,091
33		23	(a)	Sheffield U	L	1-2	Ritchie	21,468
34		30	(a)	Fulham	W	2-0	Wright 2	7,901
35	Apr	6	(h)	Blackburn R	D	0-0		15,829
36		8	(a)	Manchester C	W	2-1	Baird, Sellars	33,553
37		13	(h)	Crystal Palace	W	4-1	Baird, Sellars, Sheridan 2	12,286
38		20	(a)	Brighton & HA	D	1-1	Sellars	17,279
39		27	(h)	Oxford U	W	1-0	Baird	17,992
40	May	4	(a)	Wimbledon	D	2-2	Baird 2	6,638
41		6	(h)	Shrewsbury T	W	1-0	Baird	12,423
42		11	(a)	Birmingham C	L	0-1		24,847

FINAL LEAGUE POSITION : 7th in Division Two

Appearances

Sub Appearances

Goals

Harvey	Irwin	Hamson	Watson	Linighan	Aspin	Wright	Sheridan	McCluskey	Lorimer	Gray	Gavin	Sellars	Ritchie	Dickinson	Donnelly	Eli	Hughes	Day	Stiles	Brown	Baird	Simmonds	
1	2	3*	4	5	6	7	8	9	10	11	12												1
1	2		4	5	6	7	8	9	10	3		11											2
1	2		4	5	6	7	8	9	10	3		11											3
1	2		4	5	6	7	8	9	10	3		11											4
1	2		4*	5	6	7	8	9	10	3	12	11											5
1	2		4	5	6	7	8	9*	10	3		11	12										6
1	2		4	5	6	7	8		10	3	12	11	9										7
1	2			5		7	8		10	3	11	4	9	6									8
1	2			5		7	8		10	3	11	4	9	6									9
1	2			5		7	8	12	10	3	11*	4	9	6									10
1	2			5		7	8		10	3	11	4	9	6	12								11
1	2			5		7	8		10	3	11	4	9	6									12
1		3		5	2	7	8	9	10		11	4		6									13
1	2	3		5		7	8	9*	10		11	4	12	6									14
1	2	3		5		7	8		10	11		4	9	6									15
1	2	3		5		7	8		10	11	12	4*	9	6									16
1	2	3		5	6	7	8		10*	11		4	9			12							17
1	2	3		5	6	7	8			11		4	9	10									18
1	2	3		5	6	7	8			11		4	9	10									19
	2	3		5	6	7	8	9	10	11		4					1						20
	2	3		5	6	7	8	9	10	11		4					1						21
1	2	3		5	6	7	8	9	10	11		4											22
	2	3		5	6	7	8	12	10	11		4	9*				1						23
	2	3		5	6	7	8	12	10	11*		4	9				1						24
	2	3		5	6	7	8		10	11		4	9					1					25
	2	3		5	6	7	8	12	10	11		4*	9					1					26
	2	3		5	6	7	8	12	10	11		4*	9					1					27
	2	3		5	6	7	8	4	10	11			9					1					28
	2	3		5	6	7	8		10	11			9					1	4				29
	2	3		5	6	7	8		10	11		4	9					1					30
	2	3*		5		12	8		10	11		4	9					1		6	7		31
	2	3		5		7	8		10	11		4		6				1			9		32
	2*	3		5	6	7	8		10	11		4	12					1			9		33
	2	3		5	6	7	8	12	10	11*		4	9					1					34
	2	3		5	6	7	8	11*	10			4	9					1				12	35
	2	3		5	6	7	8		10	11		4						1			9		36
	2	3		5	6	7	8		10	11		4						1			9		37
	2	3		5	6	7	8		10	11		4						1			9		38
	2	3		5	6	7	8		10	11		4						1			9		39
	2	3		5	6	7	8		10*	11		4	12					1			9		40
	2	3		5	6	7*	8		10	11		4	12					1			9		41
	2	3		5	6*	7	8		10	11		4	12					1			9		42
20	41	31	7	42	32	41	42	13	40	39	7	39	22	12			4	18	1	1	10		
						1		6			4		6		1	1						1	
	1			2	1	14	6	5	9	1	1	7	12	1							6		

1985-86

1	Aug	17	(a)	Fulham	L	1-3	Lorimer	5,772
2		21	(h)	Wimbledon	D	0-0		12,426
3		24	(h)	Hull C	D	1-1	Baird	16,689
4		26	(a)	Stoke C	L	2-6	Aspin, Snodin	7,047
5		31	(h)	Charlton A	L	1-2	Lorimer (pen)	10,862
6	Sep	4	(a)	Brighton & HA	W	1-0	McCluskey	9,788
7		7	(a)	Shrewsbury T	W	3-1	Wright, McCluskey, Baird	4,168
8		14	(h)	Sunderland	D	1-1	Sheridan	19,693
9		21	(h)	Bradford C	W	2-1	Lorimer, Sellars	21,104
10		28	(h)	Sheffield U	D	1-1	Baird	15,622
11	Oct	5	(a)	Huddersfield T	L	1-3	Baird	9,983
12		12	(h)	Middlesbrough	W	1-0	Lorimer (pen)	14,117
13		19	(h)	Grimsby T	D	1-1	Baird	11,244
14		27	(a)	Barnsley	L	0-3		8,302
15	Nov	2	(h)	Portsmouth	W	2-1	Simmonds 2 (1 pen)	15,672
16		9	(a)	Millwall	L	1-3	Ritchie	9,158
17		16	(h)	Crystal Palace	L	1-3	McCluskey	10,378
18		23	(a)	Carlisle U	W	2-1	Linigham, Ritchie	3,504
19		30	(h)	Norwich C	L	0-2		11,480
20	Dec	7	(a)	Wimbledon	W	3-0	Snodin, Baird, Dickinson	3,492
21		14	(h)	Fulham	W	1-0	Sheridan	9,998
22		22	(a)	Hull C	L	1-2	Sheridan	11,852
23		26	(a)	Blackburn R	L	0-2		8,666
24		28	(h)	Brighton & HA	L	2-3	Baird, Snodin	13,110
25	Jan	1	(h)	Oldham A	W	3-1	Baird 2, Ritchie	10,830
26		11	(a)	Sunderland	L	2-4	Baird, Sheridan	15,139
27		18	(a)	Charlton A	L	0-4		4,333
28	Feb	1	(h)	Stoke C	W	4-0	Stiles, Baird, Swan 2	10,425
29		8	(a)	Grimsby T	L	0-1		6,382
30		15	(h)	Barnsley	L	0-2		11,765
31	Mar	8	(h)	Huddersfield T	W	2-0	Ormsby, Snodin	14,667
32		15	(a)	Middlesbrough	D	2-2	Simmonds, Rennie	6,899
33		22	(h)	Shrewsbury T	D	1-1	Rennie	9,641
34		28	(a)	Oldham A	L	1-3	Ritchie	4,937
35		31	(h)	Blackburn R	D	1-1	Ritchie	9,919
36	Apr	5	(a)	Portsmouth	W	3-2	Ritchie 2, Baird	14,430
37		9	(a)	Bradford C	W	1-0	Aspin	10,751
38		12	(h)	Millwall	W	3-1	Sellars, Swan, Ritchie	15,067
39		19	(a)	Crystal Palace	L	0-3		6,285
40		22	(a)	Sheffield U	L	2-3	Ritchie, Snodin	9,158
41		•26	(h)	Carlisle U	W	2-0	Ritchie 2	13,868
42	May	3	(a)	Norwich C	L	0-4		17,942

FINAL LEAGUE POSITION : 14th in Division Two

Appearances

Sub Appearances

Goals

Day	Irwin	Hamson	Linighan	Aspin	McCluskey	Sheridan	Baird	Lorimer	Sellars	Wright	Dickinson	Phelan	Ritchie	Swinburne	McGregor	Simmonds	Caswell	Robinson	Stiles	Thompson	Eli	Swan	Harle	Rennie	Ormsby	Taylor				
1	2	3	4	5	6	7	8	9	10	11																				1
1	2	3	4	5	6	7	8	9	10	11																				2
1	2	3	4	5	6	7	8	9	10*	11	12																			3
1	2	3	4	5	6	7*	8	9	10	11	12																			4
1	2	3	4	5	6	12	8	9*	10	11	7																			5
1	2	3	4	5	6	9	8		10		7	11																		6
1	2		4	5	6	9	8	12	10		7	11*	3																	7
1	2		4	5	6	11	8	9	10	12	7*		3																	8
1	2		4	5*	6	7	8	9	10	11	12		3																	9
1	2		4	5			8	9	10	11	7	6	3																	10
1	2		4	5		12	8	9	10	11	7	6*	3																	11
1	2	4		5	6	7	8	9	10		12		3	11*																12
	2	4		5	6	7		9	10			8	3	11	1															13
1		8	4	5	6	7		9	10			2	3	11																14
1	2	10		5	6		8	9	10				3	7		4	11													15
1		11		5	6	10	8	9				2	3	7		4														16
1		10	4	5*	6	9	8					12	3	7		2	11													17
1		10	4	5		9	8					11		7		6		2	3											18
		10	4	6		9	8					11		7	1	5	12	2	3*											19
1		10	4	6	5			9				11		7				2	3	8										20
1	2	10	4	6	5		8	9				11		7					3											21
1		10	4	5	6	9*	8					11	12	7				2	3											22
1		10	4	6*	5	9	8			12		11	3	7				2												23
1	2	10	4		5		8	9		12		11		7							3	6*								24
1	2	10	4		5			9		3		11		7									6	8						25
1	2	3	4	5	6		10	9				11		7										8						26
1	2	11	4		6		10	9				5		7				3							8					27
1		10	4		5			9						7				2	3	11			8		6					28
1		10	4		5			9				12		7				2*	3	11			8		6					29
1		10	4		5			9					12	7					3	2			8	11*	6					30
1			4		2		8	9									7		3	11			10		6	5				31
1			4		2		8	9						12			7		3*	11			10		6	5				32
1		3	4		2		8	9									7			11			10		6	5				33
1		3	4		2		8	9						11			7						10		6	5				34
1		3	4		2	7	8	9						11									10		6	5				35
1			4		2	7	8	9						11					3				10		6	5				36
1			4		2	7*	8	9						11					3	12			10		6	5				37
1			4		2					7*				9			12		3	8			10		6	5	11			38
1			4		2		8	9		12				11					3				10		6	5	7*			39
1			4		2			9		8				11					3	7			10		6	5				40
1		3	4*		2		12	9		8				7						11			10		6	5				41
1		3			2			9		8				7					4	11			10		6	5				42
40	19	30	37	24	38	20	31	34	14	13	6	17	12	28	2	5	6	8	16	11	1	1	16	3	16	12	2			
						2	1	1		4	4	2	2	1			2			1										
			5	1	2	3	4	12	4	2	1	1		11			3			1			3		2	1				

1986-87

1	Aug	23	(a)	Blackburn R	L	1-2	Ritchie	8,346
2		25	(h)	Stoke C	W	2-1	Sheridan, Baird	13,334
3		30	(h)	Sheffield U	L	0-1		18,294
4	Sep	2	(a)	Barnsley	W	1-0	Baird	6,839
5		6	(a)	Huddersfield T	D	1-1	Sheridan	8,306
6		13	(h)	Reading	W	3-2	Edwards, Ritchie, Buckley	12,248
7		20	(a)	Bradford C	L	0-2		13,525
8		27	(h)	Hull C	W	3-0	Ritchie (pen), Baird, Ormsby	13,551
9	Oct	4	(a)	Plymouth A	D	1-1	Baird	11,923
10		11	(h)	Crystal Palace	W	3-0	Sheridan (pen), Ormsby, Edwards	14,316
11		18	(h)	Portsmouth	W	3-1	Sheridan (pen), Ritchie, Baird	21,361
12		25	(a)	Grimsby T	D	0-0		7,223
13	Nov	1	(h)	Shrewsbury T	W	1-0	Aspin	14,986
14		8	(a)	Millwall	L	0-1		6,869
15		15	(h)	Oldham A	L	0-2		21,052
16		21	(a)	Birmingham C	L	1-2	Sheridan	7,836
17		29	(h)	Derby Co	W	2-0	Sheridan, Edwards	19,129
18	Dec	6	(a)	West Brom A	L	0-3		19,853
19		13	(h)	Brighton & HA	W	3-1	Sheridan, Snodin, Baird	12,014
20		21	(a)	Stoke C	L	2-7	Baird, Sheridan (pen)	12,358
21		26	(h)	Sunderland	D	1-1	Bennett (og)	21,286
22		27	(a)	Oldham A	W	1-0	Ritchie	8,477
23	Jan	1	(a)	Ipswich T	L	0-2		14,125
24		3	(h)	Huddersfield T	D	1-1	Baird	17,983
25		24	(h)	Blackburn R	D	0-0		14,452
26	Feb	7	(a)	Sheffield U	D	0-0		12,494
27		14	(h)	Barnsley	D	2-2	Baird, Sheridan	14,216
28		28	(h)	Bradford C	W	1-0	Edwards	21,802
29	Mar	7	(h)	Grimsby T	W	2-0	Ritchie, Sheridan (pen)	14,270
30		10	(a)	Portsmouth	D	1-1	Adams	13,745
31		21	(a)	Crystal Palace	L	0-1		8,781
32		28	(h)	Plymouth A	W	4-0	Sheridan (pen), Baird 3	18,618
33	Apr	4	(h)	Millwall	W	2-0	Baird, Ritchie	18,304
34		8	(a)	Hull C	D	0-0		9,531
35		14	(a)	Shrewsbury T	W	2-0	Sheridan, Pearson	4,186
36		18	(h)	Ipwsich T	W	3-2	McDonald, Sheridan, Ormsby	24,839
37		20	(a)	Sunderland	D	1-1	Pearson	14,725
38		22	(a)	Reading	L	1-2	Pearson	7,415
39		25	(h)	Birmingham C	W	4-0	Sheridan, Baird 2, Edwards	19,100
40	May	2	(a)	Derby Co	L	1-2	Ashurst	20,087
41		4	(h)	West Brom A	W	3-2	Sheridan (pen), Pearson, Ormsby	24,688
42		9	(a)	Brighton & HA	W	1-0	Edwards	8,139

FINAL LEAGUE POSITION : 4th in Division Two

Appearances

Sub Appearances

Goals

Sinclair	Haddock	Caswell	Snodin	Ormsby	Rennie	Ritchie	Stiles	Baird	Edwards	Ashurst	Swan	Aspin	Thompson	Sheridan	Buckley	Day	Robinson	Taylor	Doig	Adams	Pearson	McDonald	Aizlewood	
1	2	3	4	5*	6	7	8	9	10	11	12													1
1			4		6	11	7	9	10	5		2	3	8										2
1	3		4		6	11	7	9	10	5		2		8										3
1	3		4		6	11	7	9	10	5		2		8										4
1	3				6	11	7*	9	10	5	4	2		8	12									5
1	3				6	11	7	9	10	5	4*	3		8	12									6
1	3		4*		6	11	7		10	5	12	2		8	9									7
	3			4	6	11	7	9	10	5		2		8		1								8
	3			4	6	11	7	9	10	5		2		8		1								9
				4	6	11	7	9	10	5		2		8		1	3							10
				4	6	11	7	9	10	5		2		8		1	3							11
				4	6	11	7*	9	10	5		2	12	8		1	3							12
1	7*			4	6	11		9	10	5		2		8	12		3							13
	12		4	6	7*	11		9	10	5		2		8		1	3							14
			4	6		11		9		5		2		8	7	1	3	10						15
			4	6				9	10	5		2	7	8		1	3	11						16
			4	6		11	7	9	10	5		2		8*		1	3		12					17
			4	6	11*	12	7	9	10	5		2		8		1	3							18
			4	6	11		12	9	10	5		2		8		1	3		7*					19
					11	12		9	10	5	6	2	4	8		1	3*		7					20
					3	11		9	10	5	6	2	4	8	7	1								21
			4	6	11	10	3	9			5	2		8	7	1								22
			4	6	11	10	3	9	12	5		2		8	7*	1								23
			4	6	11	7	3	9	10	5		2		8		1								24
				6	8	7	4	10		5		2			11*	1			12	3	9			25
				6			7	10		5		2		8		1				11	9	3	4	26
				6			7*	10	12	5		2		8		1				11	9	3	4	27
				6		7	11*	10	12	5		2		8		1					9	3	4	28
					6	7			10	5		2		8		1				11	9	3	4	29
				6			7	10		5		2		8		1				11	9	3	4	30
				6			7	10		5		2		8		1				11	9	3	4	31
				6		7		10	12	5		2		8*		1				11	9	3	4	32
				6		7		10		5		2		8		1				11	9	3	4	33
				6		7	12	10		5		2		8		1				11	9	3	4*	34
				6		7		10		5		2		8		1				11	9	3	4	35
				6		7		10		5		2		8		1				11	9	3	4	36
				6		7*	12	10		5		2		8		1				11	9	3	4	37
				6				10	7	5		2		8		1				11	9	3	4	38
				6				10	7	5		2		8		1				11	9	3	4	39
				6	4*		7	10	12	5		2		8		1				11	9	3		40
				6			7	10		5		2		8		1				11	9	3	4	41
	4			6			7	10	12	5		2		8		1				11	9*	3		42
8	10	1	14	33	24	29	26	40	24	41	5	41	4	40	6	34	11	2	2	17	18	17	15	
	1					2	3		6		2		1		3				2					
			1	4		7		15	6	1		1		15	1					1	4	1		

1987-88

1	Aug	16	(a)	Barnsley	D	1-1	Taylor	9,778
2		19	(h)	Leicester C	W	1-0	Sheridan (pen)	21,034
3		22	(h)	Reading	D	0-0		19,286
4		29	(a)	Bradford C	D	0-0		11,428
5		31	(h)	West Brom A	W	1-0	Sheridan	19,847
6	Sep	5	(a)	Ipswich T	L	0-1		11,163
7		12	(h)	Hull C	L	0-2		18,205
8		15	(a)	Huddersfield T	D	0-0		9,085
9		19	(a)	Middlesbrough	L	0-2		12,051
10		26	(h)	Manchester C	W	2-0	De Mange, Snodin	25,358
11		30	(h)	Stoke C	D	0-0		17,208
12	Oct	3	(a)	Blackburn R	D	1-1	Taylor	7,675
13		10	(h)	Aston Villa	L	1-3	Taylor	20,741
14		17	(a)	Plymouth A	L	3-6	Taylor, Snodin 2	9,358
15		20	(a)	Oldham A	D	1-1	Swan	6,312
16		24	(h)	Bournemouth	W	3-2	Taylor, Swan, Rennie	15,253
17		31	(a)	Sheffield U	D	2-2	Snodin, Swan	12,095
18	Nov	7	(h)	Shrewsbury T	W	2-1	Stiles, Taylor	13,760
19		14	(a)	Millwall	L	1-3	McLeary (og)	8,014
20		21	(h)	Swindon T	W	4-2	Rennie, Davison, Taylor, Haddock	15,457
21		28	(a)	Crystal Palace	L	0-3		8,749
22	Dec	5	(h)	Birmingham C	W	4-1	Sheridan (pen), Davison, Swan, Taylor	15,977
23		12	(a)	Reading	W	1-0	Sheridan (pen)	6,505
24		19	(h)	Huddersfield T	W	3-0	Sheridan 2, Davison	20,111
25		26	(a)	Manchester C	W	2-1	Redmond (og), Batty	30,153
26		28	(h)	Middlesbrough	W	2-0	Davison, Swan	34,186
27	Jan	1	(h)	Bradford C	W	2-0	Williams, Snodin	36,004
28		3	(a)	Hull C	L	1-3	Swan	14,694
29		16	(h)	Barnsley	L	0-2		19,028
30		30	(a)	West Brom A	W	4-1	Sheridan, Williams, Pearson, Davison	9,008
31	Feb	6	(h)	Ipswich T	W	1-0	Pearson	19,564
32		13	(a)	Leicester C	L	2-3	Williams, Sheridan (pen)	11,937
33		23	(a)	Stoke C	L	1-2	Pearson	10,129
34		27	(h)	Blackburn R	D	2-2	Sheridan (pen), Snodin	23,843
35	Mar	5	(h)	Plymouth A	W	1-0	Baird	18,115
36		12	(a)	Aston Villa	W	2-1	Swan, Taylor	19,677
37		19	(h)	Sheffield U	W	5-0	Swan, Pearson 3, Sheridan	22,376
38		26	(a)	Bournemouth	D	0-0		8,147
39	Apr	2	(a)	Shrewsbury T	L	0-1		7,369
40		6	(h)	Millwall	L	1-2	Sheridan (pen)	24,241
41		23	(h)	Oldham A	D	1-1	Snodin	13,442
42		30	(a)	Swindon T	W	2-1	Baird 2	8,299
43	May	2	(h)	Crystal Palace	W	1-0	Sheridan (pen)	13,217
44		6	(a)	Birmingham C	D	0-0		6,024

FINAL LEAGUE POSITION : 7th in Division Two

Appearances

Sub Appearances

Goals

Day	Aspin	Adams	Aizlewood	Ashurst	Rennie	Williams	Sheridan	Pearson	Taylor	Snodin	Edwards	Haddock	Buckley	Doig	Stiles	Grayson	Mumby	De Mange	Melrose	Swan	McDonald	Batty	Davison	Baird	Brockie	Maguire	Noteman			
1	2	3	4	5	6	7	8	9	10*	11	12																			1
1	2	3	4	5	6	7	8	9	10*	11†	12	14																		2
1	2	3	4	5	6	7	8	9*			10	11	12																	3
1	2	3	4	5	6	7	8	9	10			11																		4
1	2	3	4	5	6	7*	8	14	10		9†	11		12																5
1	2	3	4	5	6	7	8	12	10*		9	11																		6
1	2	3	4*	5	6		8	9		11	10	12			7															7
1	2	3		5	6		8	9		7*	12	11			14	4†	10													8
1	2	3		5	6		8	9	10*	11	12	4†			14		7													9
1	2	3		5	6*		8	14	10	11		4					12	7	9†											10
1	2	3		5	6		8	12	10	11		4						7	9*											11
1	2	3		5	6		8	10	12	11		4						7	9*											12
1	14	3		5	6		8		9*	11		2			4†		10	7	12											13
1	2	3*		5		6	8	10†	9	11		4			12			7		14										14
1	2	3		5		8		10*	9	11		6			4			7		12										15
1		3		5	6	4	8		9	11		2						7		10										16
1		3		5		2	8		9	11		6		7				4		10										17
1				5	7	2			9	11		6			8			4		10	3									18
1				5	3	2		7	9	11		6			8			4		10										19
1		3		5	8	2*			9	11		6			12			4				7	10							20
1		3		5	8*	2			9	11		6						4		12		7	10							21
1	2	3		5		4	8		9	11		6								12		7	10*							22
1	2	3		5			8		9			6						4		11		7	10							23
1	2	3		5		4	8		9			6								11		7	10							24
1	2	3		5		4	8			11*		6			12					9		7	10							25
1	2	3		5		4	8			11		6								9		7	10							26
1	2	3		5		4	8			11		6								9		7	10							27
1	2	3		5		4	8*		14	11†		6			12					9		7	10							28
1	2	3		5		4	8		9†			6					14	12		11		7*	10							29
1	2	3		5	11*	4	8	9	12			6						7					10							30
1	2	3		5	7	4	8	9		11		6											10							31
1	2	3		5	7	4	8	9	12			6*										11	10							32
1		3	4	5		2	8	9		11		6										7								33
1		3	4	5	12	2	8	9	10	11		6*										7								34
1		3	4	5	12	2*	8	10		11										6		7		9						35
1			4*	5	12	2		10	8	11		3								6		7		9						36
1			4*	5		2	12	10	8	11		3								6		7		9						37
1		3	4	5		2	12	10		11†		8*								6		7	14	9						38
1		3	4	5		2†	8	10*	11	14		7								6		12		9						39
1		3	4	5			8	12	11†	14		2								6		7	10*	9						40
1		3	4	5	10		8		12	11		2								6*		7		9						41
1		3			6		8	12	10*	11		2			4					5		7		9						42
1		3	14		6		8	12		11					4*					5		7		9	2	10†				43
1		3*			6		8			11						4				5		7		9	2	10	12			44
44	25	40	16	41	25	31	36	21	27	33	4	38		1	7	2	3	14	3	21	1	22	15	10	2	2				
	1		1		3		2	7	5	2	4	2	1	1	6		2	1	1	4		1	1				1			
					2	3	12	6	9	7		1			1			1		8		1	5	3						

1988-89

1	Aug	27	(h)	Oxford U	D	1-1	Snodin	20,697
2	Sep	3	(a)	Portsmouth	L	0-4		15,263
3		10	(h)	Manchester C	D	1-1	Blake	23,122
4		17	(a)	Bournemouth	D	0-0		7,922
5		21	(h)	Barnsley	W	2-0	Davison, Hilaire	17,390
6		24	(h)	Chelsea	L	0-2		26,080
7	Oct	1	(a)	Brighton & HA	L	1-2	Baird	7,109
8		4	(a)	Sunderland	L	1-2	Davison	12,671
9		8	(h)	Watford	L	0-1		15,657
10		16	(a)	Swindon T	D	0-0		9,234
11		22	(h)	Leicester C	D	1-1	Hilaire	17,263
12		26	(a)	Bradford C	D	1-1	Davison	13,048
13		29	(h)	Hull C	W	2-1	Sheridan, Baird	17,536
14	Nov	5	(a)	Ipswich T	W	1-0	Sheridan (pen)	11,755
15		12	(h)	West Brom A	W	2-1	Aizlewood, Baird	20,442
16		19	(a)	Oldham A	D	2-2	Davison 2	8,824
17		22	(a)	Birmingham C	D	0-0		6,168
18		26	(h)	Stoke C	W	4-0	Baird 2, Davison, Sheridan (pen)	19,933
19	Dec	3	(a)	Walsall	W	3-0	Davison 2, Whitlow	6,886
20		10	(h)	Shrewsbury T	L	2-3	Sheridan (pen), Davison	19,987
21		17	(a)	Crystal Palace	D	0-0		9,847
22		26	(h)	Blackburn R	W	2-0	Baird, Davison	31,622
23		31	(h)	Plymouth A	W	2-0	Baird, Snodin	24,043
24	Jan	2	(a)	Manchester C	D	0-0		33,034
25		14	(h)	Birmingham C	W	1-0	Hilaire	21,837
26		21	(a)	Oxford U	L	2-3	Blake, Hilaire	7,926
27	Feb	4	(h)	Sunderland	W	2-0	Davison, Sheridan (pen)	31,984
28		11	(a)	Watford	D	1-1	Pearson	13,439
29		18	(a)	Leicester C	W	2-1	Davison, Snodin	14,151
30		25	(h)	Swindon T	D	0-0		22,651
31	Mar	1	(h)	Bradford C	D	3-3	Blake, Hilaire, Baird	33,325
32		5	(a)	West Brom A	L	1-2	Adams	15,914
33		11	(h)	Ipswich T	L	2-4	Hilaire, Blake	19,639
34		14	(a)	Hull C	W	2-1	Baird, Davison	8,887
35		19	(a)	Barnsley	D	2-2	Aizlewood, Sheridan (pen)	11,578
36		25	(h)	Portsmouth	W	1-0	Baird	27,049
37		27	(a)	Blackburn R	L	0-2		11,533
38	Apr	1	(h)	Bournemouth	W	3-0	Shutt 3	21,095
39		5	(h)	Crystal Palace	L	1-2	Shutt	25,604
40		9	(a)	Plymouth A	L	0-1		9,365
41		15	(h)	Brighton & HA	W	1-0	Williams A	14,915
42		22	(a)	Chelsea	L	0-1		30,332
43		29	(a)	Stoke C	W	3-2	Sheridan (pen), Davison, Strachan	9,051
44	May	1	(h)	Walsall	W	1-0	Aizlewood	13,280
45		6	(h)	Oldham A	D	0-0		14,459
46		13	(a)	Shrewsbury T	D	3-3	Strachan 2 (1 pen), Rennie	4,693

FINAL LEAGUE POSITION: 10th in Division Two

Appearances

Sub Appearances

Goals

Day	Haddock	Adams	Aizlewood	Blake	Ashurst	Stiles	Hilaire	Baird	Pearson	Snodin	Davison	Rennie	Taylor	Williams G	Batty	Sheridan	Aspin	Williams A	Whitlow	Andrews	Swan	Fairclough	Strachan	Shutt	Kerr	Speed	Mumby	Ormsby		
1	2	3	4	5	6	7†	8	9	10*	11	12	14																		1
1	2	3	4	5	6	8	11	9	10		12		7*																	2
1		3†	4	5	6		11	9	12		10*			2	7	8	14													3
1	14	3	4	5	6		11		12		10		9*	2	7	8†														4
1	12	3	4*	5	6		11	9			10			2	7	8														5
1	4*	3		5	6		11	9†	14	12	10			2	7	8														6
1		3	4*	5			11	9	10	8		6		2	7	12														7
1	2†	3		5		4	11	9*	12		10	6			7	8	14													8
1		3		5		4†	11	9	12	14	10*	6			7	8	2													9
1			4	5	14		11	9	12	3	10*	6			7†	8	2													10
1			4	5		14	11	9	12	3	10*	6			7†	8	2													11
1			4	5		14	11	9*	12	3	10	6			7	8†	2													12
1			4	5		14	11†	9	12	3	10*	6			7	8	2													13
1			4	5		14	11†	9	12	3	10	6			7	8*	2													14
1			4	5			11	9	12	3†	10*	6			7	8	2	14												15
1			4	5			11	9	12	3	10*	6			7†	8	2	14												16
1		12	4	5			11	9		3	10†	6	14			8	2	7*												17
1			4	5			11	9		3	10	6			12	8*	2		7											18
1			4	5			11*	9		3	10	6				8	2	12	7											19
1			4	5			11	9*		3	10	6	12			8	2		7											20
			4	5			11†	9		3	10*	6	12			8	2	14	7	1										21
1			4	5			11†	9	12	3	10*	6				8	2	14	7											22
1			4	5			11	9	12	3	10*	6				8	2		7											23
1			4	5			11†	9*	12	3	10	6			14	8	2		7											24
1			4	5			11	9	12	3	10*	6					2	8	7											25
1			4	5			11	9*	12	3	10	6				8	2	14	7†											26
1		4		5			11	9		3	10	6			7	8	2													27
1		4		5			11	9	12	3	10*	6			7	8	2†	14												28
1		4	14	5			11	9†	12	3	10	6			7	8*	2													29
1		4	14	5			11	9*	12	3†	10	6			7	8	2													30
1		4*	12	5			11	9		3	10	6			7	8	2													31
1		4†	14	5			11	9	12	3	10*	6		2	7	8														32
1			4	5			11	9	12	3	10*	6†		2	7	8			14											33
1			4				11†	9	12	3	10*			2	7	8	6		14		5									34
1	2		4	5			11†		9	3	10*		12			8	6	14	7											35
1			4	5			11	9	12	3	10†					8*	2	14				6	7							36
1			4	5			11†	9	10	3					12	8*	2	14				6	7							37
1			4	5				9		3*						8	2	12	11			6	7	10						38
1			4				11*	9	12	3		5				8	2					6	7	10						39
1				5				9	12	3†		14			8		2	4	11			6	7	10*						40
1	2†		3	5					9		10	14				8		4	11*			6	7		12					41
1			4	5				9	12		10					14	2*	8	11			6	7		3†					42
1	14		4*	5			11	9†			10				12	8		2	3			6	7							43
1	14		4*	5			11	9			10†				12	8		2	3			6	7							44
1	2			5		14	11	9				4†			8				3*			6	7			10	12			45
1	2			5		14	11	9†				10			8				3*			6	7		12			4		46
45	8	15	34	44	6	4	42	43	6	33	37	30	2	8	25	38	31	7	18	1	1	11	11	3	1	1		1		
	4	1	4		1	6			27	2	2	3	4		5	2	2	11	2						2		1			
		1	3	4			6	10	1	3	14	1				7		1	1				3	4						

1989-90

1	Aug	19	(a)	Newcastle U	L	2-5	Davison, Baird	24,482
2		23	(h)	Middlesbrough	W	2-1	Davison, Parkinson (og)	25,004
3		26	(h)	Blackburn R	D	1-1	Fairclough	25,045
4	Sep	2	(a)	Stoke C	D	1-1	Strachan	14,570
5		9	(h)	Ipswich T	D	1-1	Jones	22,972
6		16	(a)	Hull C	W	1-0	Davison	11,620
7		23	(h)	Swindon T	W	4-0	Strachan 3 (1 pen), Davison	21,694
8		27	(h)	Oxford U	W	2-1	Davison, Sterland	24,097
9		30	(a)	Port Vale	D	0-0		11,156
10	Oct	7	(a)	West Ham U	W	1-0	Jones	23,539
11		14	(h)	Sunderland	W	2-0	Davison, Fairclough	27,815
12		17	(a)	Portsmouth	D	3-3	Davison, Whitlow, Sterland	10,260
13		21	(h)	Wolverhampton W	W	1-0	Davison	28,204
14		28	(a)	Bradford C	W	1-0	Davison	12,527
15	Nov	1	(h)	Plymouth A	W	2-1	Strachan (pen), Davison	26,791
16		4	(h)	Bournemouth	W	3-0	Baird, Strachan (pen), Fairclough	26,484
17		11	(a)	Leicester C	L	3-4	Baird, Williams, Strachan (pen)	18,032
18		18	(h)	Watford	W	2-1	Fairclough, Williams	26,921
19		25	(a)	West Brom A	L	1-2	Fairclough	15,116
20	Dec	2	(h)	Newcastle U	W	1-0	Baird	31,715
21		9	(a)	Middlesbrough	W	2-0	Shutt, Fairclough	19,686
22		16	(h)	Brighton & HA	W	3-0	Strachan, Hendrie, Jones	24,070
23		26	(a)	Sheffield U	D	2-2	Sterland, Shutt	31,602
24		30	(a)	Barnsley	L	0-1		14,841
25	Jan	1	(h)	Oldham A	D	1-1	Hendrie	30,217
26		13	(a)	Blackburn R	W	2-1	Chapman, Strachan	14,485
27		20	(h)	Stoke C	W	2-0	Strachan (pen), Hendrie	29,318
28	Feb	4	(a)	Swindon T	L	2-3	Strachan (pen), Hendrie	16,208
29		10	(h)	Hull C	W	4-3	Hendrie, Jones, Varadi, Strachan	29,977
30		17	(a)	Ipswich T	D	2-2	Chapman 2	17,102
31		24	(h)	West Brom A	D	2-2	Kamara, Chapman	30,004
32	Mar	3	(a)	Watford	L	0-1		13,468
33		7	(h)	Port Vale	D	0-0		28,756
34		10	(a)	Oxford U	W	4-2	Chapman 2, Varadi, Fairclough	8,397
35		17	(h)	West Ham U	W	3-2	Chapman 2, Strachan	32,536
36		20	(a)	Sunderland	W	1-0	Sterland	17,851
37		24	(h)	Portsmouth	W	2-0	Jones, Chapman	27,600
38		31	(a)	Wolverhampton W	L	0-1		22,419
39	Apr	7	(h)	Bradford C	D	1-1	Speed	32,316
40		10	(a)	Plymouth A	D	1-1	Chapman	11,382
41		13	(a)	Oldham A	L	1-3	Davison	16,292
42		16	(h)	Sheffield U	W	4-0	Strachan2 (1 pen), Chapman, Speed	32,727
43		21	(a)	Brighton & HA	D	2-2	Speed, Chapman (og)	11,359
44		25	(h)	Barnsley	L	1-2	Fairclough	31,700
45		28	(h)	Leicester C	W	2-1	Sterland, Strachan	32,597
46	May	5	(a)	Bournemouth	W	1-0	Chapman	9,918

FINAL LEAGUE POSITION: 1st in Division Two

Appearances

Sub Appearances

Goals

Day	Sterland	Beglin	Thomas	McClelland	Haddock	Strachan	Batty	Baird	Davison	Hendrie	Shutt	Whitlow	Fairclough	Jones	Speed	Blake	Williams A	Turner	Pearson	Kerr	Snodin	Chapman	Kamara	O'Donnell	Hilaire	Varadi				
1	2	3	4†	5	6	7	8	9	10*	11	12	14																		1
1	2		4*		6	7	8	9†	10	11	12	3	5	14																2
1	2		4†		6	7	8	9	10*	11	12	3	5	14																3
1	2				6	7	8	9	10*	11		3	5	4	12															4
1	2				6	7	8	9	10	11*		3	5	4	12															5
1	2					7	8	9	10	11*		3	6	4		5	12													6
1	2				6	7	8	9	10	11*		3		4		5	12													7
1	2				6	7	8	9	10	11		3		4*		5	12													8
1	2				6	7	8	9	10*		12	3		4†	14	5	11													9
1	2				6	7	8	9	10*		12	3	5	4			11													10
1	2				6	7	8	9	10			3	5	4			11													11
1	2				6	7	8	9	10			3	5	4			11													12
1	2				6	7†	8	9	10		12	3	5	4	14		11*													13
1	2				6	7	8	9	10			3	5	4	12		11*													14
1	2				6	7	8	9	10			3	5	4*	12		11													15
1	2				6	7	8	9	10			3	5	4	12		11*													16
1*	2				6	7	8	9	10		12	3	5	4			11													17
	2				6	7	8	9	10*		12	3	5	4			11	1												18
	2				6	7	8	9	10		12	3	5	4*	14		11†	1												19
1	2					7	8	9	10		12	3	6	4		5	11*													20
1	2					7	8				10	3	6	4		5	11		9											21
1	2				6	7	8	12		11†	10*	3	5	4	14				9											22
1	2					7	8	9		11	10	3	6	4		5														23
1	2				6	7	8	9		11*	10	3†	5	4					12	14										24
1	2				6	7	8	9*		11	10†		5	4					12	3	14									25
1	2*	12			6	7	8		10	11		3	5	4								9								26
1		2			6	7	8		10*	11		3	5	4					12			9								27
1		2			6	7	8			11		3*	5	4	14				12	10†		9								28
1		3†			6	7	8			11			5	4								9*	2	14	12	10				29
1		3			6	7	8			11*			5	4								9	2		12	10				30
1	12	3			6	7	8			11			5	4								9	2			10*				31
1	2	3			6	7	8			12			5	4	14							9	11†			10*				32
1	2	3			6	7	8			11*			5	4	12							9				10				33
1	2	3*			6	7				12			5	4	8†					14	11	9				10				34
1	2				6	7				11†	12		5	4	8					14	3	9				10*				35
1	2				6	7	8		14	12			5	4	11						3*	9				10†				36
1	2	3			6	7*	8			12		14	5	4	11							9				10†				37
1	2				6	7	8			12		3	5	4	11*							9	14			10†				38
1	2	3			6	7	8		12	10*			5	4	11							9								39
1	2	3			6	7	8		12	10*			5	4	11							9								40
1	2	3			6*	7	8		14				5	4	12							9	11			10†				41
1	2	3		6		7			10*		12		5	4	11							9	8							42
1	2	3		6		7	14				12		5	4	11							9	8†			10*				43
1	2	3			6	7					10*		5	4	11				12			9	8							44
1	2	3			6	7	14		10*				5	4†	11							9	8			12				45
1	2	3			6	7	14		10*		12†		5	4	11							9	8							46
44	41	18	3	3	40	46	39	23	25	22	6	27	42	43	12	7	13	2	2	2	3	21	10			12				
	1	1					3	1	4	5	14	2		2	13		3		5	3	1		1	1	2	1				
	5					16		4	11	5	2	1	8	5	3		2					12	1			2				

1990-91

1	Aug	25	(a)	Everton	W	3-2	Fairclough, Speed, Varadi	34,412
2		28	(h)	Manchester U	D	0-0		29,172
3	Sep	1	(h)	Norwich C	W	3-0	Chapman 2, Varadi	25,684
4		8	(a)	Luton T	L	0-1		10,185
5		15	(h)	Tottenham H	L	0-2		31,342
6		23	(a)	Sheffield U	W	2-0	Pearson, Strachan	26,078
7		29	(h)	Arsenal	D	2-2	Chapman, Strachan (pen)	30,085
8	Oct	6	(a)	Crystal Palace	D	1-1	Speed	21,676
9		20	(h)	QPR	L	2-3	Whyte, Chapman	27,443
10		27	(a)	Aston Villa	D	0-0		24,219
11	Nov	3	(h)	Nottingham F	W	3-1	Chapman, Strachan (pen), McAllister	30,409
12		11	(a)	Manchester C	W	3-2	Chapman, Shutt, Strachan	27,782
13		17	(h)	Derby Co	W	3-0	Chapman, Strachan, Speed	27,868
14		24	(a)	Coventry C	D	1-1	Chapman	16,183
15	Dec	1	(h)	Southampton	W	2-1	Fairclough, Shutt	29,341
16		8	(a)	Manchester U	D	1-1	Sterland	40,927
17		16	(h)	Everton	W	2-0	Strachan (pen), Shutt	27,775
18		23	(a)	Sunderland	W	1-0	Sterland	23,773
19		26	(h)	Chelsea	W	4-1	Sterland, Chapman 2, Whitlow	30,893
20		29	(h)	Wimbledon	W	3-0	Chapman, Speed, Sterland	29,292
21	Jan	1	(a)	Liverpool	L	0-3		36,975
22		12	(a)	Norwich C	L	0-2		17,786
23		19	(h)	Luton T	W	2-1	Strachan (pen), Fairclough	27,010
24	Feb	2	(a)	Tottenham H	D	0-0		32,253
25	Mar	2	(a)	Southampton	L	0-2		16,858
26		9	(h)	Coventry C	W	2-0	Davison, Whyte	28,880
27		17	(a)	Arsenal	L	0-2		26,218
28		23	(h)	Crystal Palace	L	1-2	Speed	28,556
29		30	(a)	Chelsea	W	2-1	Shutt, Fairclough	17,585
30	Apr	2	(h)	Sunderland	W	5-0	Chapman 2, Shutt, Speed 2	28,132
31		6	(a)	Wimbledon	W	1-0	Chapman	6,800
32		10	(h)	Manchester C	L	1-2	McAllister	28,757
33		13	(h)	Liverpool	L	4-5	Chapman 3, Shutt	31,460
34		17	(a)	QPR	L	0-2		10,998
35		23	(a)	Derby Co	W	1-0	Shutt	12,666
36	May	4	(h)	Aston Villa	W	5-2	Price (og), Chapman 2, Whyte, Shutt	29,188
37		8	(h)	Sheffield U	W	2-1	Sterland, Shutt	28,978
38		11	(a)	Nottingham F	L	3-4	Chapman 2, Shutt	25,067

FINAL LEAGUE POSITION: 4th in Division One

Appearances

Sub Appearances

Goals

Lukic	Sterland	Snodin	Batty	Fairclough	Whyte	Strachan	Varadi	Chapman	McAllister	Speed	Kamara	Haddock	Whitlow	Jones	Pearson	Shutt	Williams	Davison	McClelland	
1	2	3	4	5	6	7	8*	9	10	11†	12	14								1
1	2	12	4	5	6	7	8	9	10	11*		3								2
1	2	3*	4	5	6	7	8	9	10†	11		14	12							3
1	2	3†	4		6	7	12	9	10	14		5	11	8*						4
1	2	12	4	5	6	7	8	9	10	11*		14	3†							5
1	2		4	5	6	7	8*	9	10	11		3			12					6
1	2	11*	4	5	6	7		9	10	12		3			8					7
1	2		4	5	6	7		9	10	11		3			8					8
1	2	3	4	5	6	7		9	10*	11	12				8†	14				9
1	2		4	5	6	7		9	10	11	3				8					10
1	2	12	4	5	6	7		9	10	11	3					8*				11
1	2		4	5	6	7		9	10	11	3				12	8*				12
1	2		4	5	6	7		9	10	11	3					8				13
1	2		4	6	5	7		9	10	11	3†	14			12	8*				14
1	2		4	5	6	7		9*	10†	11		3			12	8	14			15
1	2		4	5	6	7		9	10	11		3				8				16
1	2	12	4	5	6	7		9	10	11*		3				8				17
1	2	12	4	5	6	7		9	10	11		3*				8				18
1	2	3	4	5	6	7		9	10	11*			12			8				19
1	2	3*	4	5	6	7		9	10	11			12		14	8†				20
1	2	3*	4	5	6	7		9	10	11			12		14	8†				21
1	2	3	4	5	6	7		9	10	12			11*		14	8†				22
1	2	3*	4	5	6	7		9	10	11		12				8				23
1	2	12		5	6	7		9†	10	11		3	4		14*		8			24
1	2		4	5	6			9	10	11			3			8	7*	12		25
1	2		4	5	6	7		9	10	11			3			12		8*		26
1	2		4	5	6	7		9	10	11			3			12		8*		27
1	2		4	5	6	7		9	10†	11			3		14	8*	12			28
1	2		4	5	6	7*		9	10	11			3			8	12			29
1	2		4		6	7		9	10	11			3			8			5	30
1	2		4		6	7		9	10	11			3			8*	12		5	31
1	2		4		6			9	10	11			3			8	7*	12	5	32
1	2		4	5	6	7		9	10	11			3			8				33
1	2		4	5	6	7		9	10	11			3*			8	12			34
1	2	3*	4	5	6	7		9	10	11						8	12			35
1	2	3	4	5	6			9	10	11						8	7*	12		36
1	2	3	4	5	6			9	10	11						8	7			37
1	2	3	4	5	6	7*		9	10	11						8	12			38
38	38	14	37	34	38	34	5	38	38	35	5	10	14	1	4	25	5	2	3	
		6					1			3	2	5	4		9	3	7	3		
	5			4	3	7	2	21	2	7			1		1	10		1		

1991-92

1	Aug	20	(h)	Nottingham F	W	1-0	McAllister	29,457
2		24	(h)	Sheffield W	D	1-1	Hodge	30,260
3		28	(a)	Southampton	W	4-0	Speed 2, Strachan 2 (2 pens)	15,847
4		31	(a)	Manchester U	D	1-1	Chapman	43,778
5	Sep	3	(h)	Arsenal	D	2-2	Strachan (pen), Chapman	29,396
6		7	(h)	Manchester C	W	3-0	Dorigo, Batty, Strachan (pen)	29,986
7		14	(a)	Chelsea	W	1-0	Shutt	23,439
8		18	(a)	Coventry C	D	0-0		15,488
9		21	(h)	Liverpool	W	1-0	Hodge	32,917
10		28	(a)	Norwich C	D	2-2	Dorigo, Speed	15,828
11	Oct	1	(a)	Crystal Palace	L	0-1		18,298
12		5	(h)	Sheffield U	W	4-3	Hodge 2, Sterland 2 (1 pen)	28,362
13		19	(a)	Notts Co	W	4-2	Chapman, Hodge, Whyte, McAllister	12,964
14		26	(h)	Oldham A	W	1-0	Kilcline (og)	28,199
15	Nov	2	(a)	Wimbledon	D	0-0		7,025
16		16	(h)	QPR	W	2-0	Sterland, Wallace	27,087
17		24	(a)	Aston Villa	W	4-1	Wallace, Sterland, Chapman 2	23,666
18		30	(h)	Everton	W	1-0	Wallace	30,043
19	Dec	7	(a)	Luton T	W	2-0	Wallace, Speed	11,550
20		14	(h)	Tottenham H	D	1-1	Speed	31,404
21		22	(a)	Nottingham F	D	0-0		27,170
22		26	(h)	Southampton	D	3-3	Hodge 2, Speed	29,053
23		29	(h)	Manchester U	D	1-1	Sterland (pen)	32,638
24	Jan	1	(a)	West Ham U	W	3-1	Chapman 2, McAllister	21,766
25		12	(a)	Sheffield W	W	6-1	Chapman 3, Dorigo, Whitlow, Wallace	32,228
26		18	(h)	Crystal Palace	D	1-1	Fairclough	27,717
27	Feb	1	(h)	Notts Co	W	3-0	Sterland, Batty, Wallace	27,224
28		8	(a)	Oldham A	L	0-2		18,409
29		23	(a)	Everton	D	1-1	Keown (og)	19,248
30		29	(h)	Luton T	W	2-0	Cantona, Chapman	28,231
31	Mar	3	(h)	Aston Villa	D	0-0		28,896
32		7	(a)	Tottenham H	W	3-1	Wallace, Newsome, McAllister	27,622
33		11	(a)	QPR	L	1-4	Speed	14,641
34		14	(h)	Wimbledon	W	5-1	Chapman 3, Wallace, Cantona	26,760
35		22	(a)	Arsenal	D	1-1	Chapman	27,844
36		28	(h)	West Ham U	D	0-0		31,101
37	Apr	4	(a)	Manchester C	L	0-4		30,239
38		11	(h)	Chelsea	W	3-0	Wallace, Chapman, Cantona	31,363
39		18	(a)	Liverpool	D	0-0		37,186
40		20	(h)	Coventry C	W	2-0	Fairclough, McAllister (pen)	26,582
41		26	(a)	Sheffield U	W	3-2	Wallace, Newsome, Gayle (og)	32,000
42	May	2	(h)	Norwich C	W	1-0	Wallace	32,673

FINAL LEAGUE POSITION: 1st in Division One

Appearances

Sub Appearances

Goals

Lukic	McClelland	Dorigo	Batty	Fairclough	Whyte	Strachan	Wallace	Chapman	McAllister	Speed	Hodge	Sterland	Wetherall	Shutt	Varadi	Whitlow	Kamara	Newsome	Kelly	Davison	Cantona	Agana	
1	2	3	4	5	6	7	8	9	10	11													1
1	2†	3	4	5	6	7	8	9	10	11*	12	14											2
1	2	3	4	5†	6	7	8	9	10*	11	12	14											3
1	5	3	4		6	7	8	9	10*	11	12	2											4
1	5	3†	4		6	7	8	9	10	11	12	2*	14										5
1	5	3	4		6	7	8*	9	10	11	12	2											6
1	5	3	4		6	7*		9	10	11	12	2		8									7
1	5	3	4		6	7		9	10	11	12	2		8*									8
1	5	3	4		6	7		9	10	11*	8	2		12									9
1	5	3	4		6			9	10	11	8†	2		12	7*	14							10
1	5	3	4		6			9	10†	11	8	2		12	7*	14							11
1	5	3	4	12	6			9	10†	11	7	2*		8		14							12
1		3	4	5	6	7		9*	12†	11	10	2		8			14						13
1		3	4	5	6	7*	8	9	10	11†		2		12			14						14
1		3		5	6	7	8*	9	10	11		2		4				12					15
1		3	4	5	6	7	8	9	10	11*		2			12								16
1	11	3	4	5	6	7	8	9	10			2											17
1	14	3	4	5	6	7	8	9	10	11*	12†	2											18
1		3	4	5	6	7	8	9	10	11		2											19
1	5	3	4		6	7	8	9	10	11		2											20
1	5	3	4		6	7*	8	9	10	11		2							12				21
1	5	3	4		6		8	9	10	11	7	2											22
1		3	4*	5	6	7	8	9	10	11	12	2											23
1		3	4	5	6	7	8	9	10	11		2											24
1		3		5	6		8	9	10	11	4†	2		7*		12				14			25
1		3	4	5	6	7	8		10†	11	9*	2				12				14			26
1		3	4	5	6	7†	8		10	11	9	2*				12			14				27
1		3	4	5	6	7	8		10	11	9†	2*				12					14		28
1		3	4	5	6	7	8*		10	11		2		12							9		29
1		3*	4	5	6	7	8†	9	10	11		2									12	14	30
1	14		4	5†	6	7		9	10	11		2				3					12	8*	31
1			4	5	6	7	8	9	10	11		2†				3*		14			12		32
1			4	5	6	7	8	9	10*	11						3		2			12		33
1			4	5	6	7*	8	9	10	11				12				2			3		34
1		3	4	5	6	7	8	9	10	11											2		35
1		3	4	5		7	8*	9	10	11	12							6			2		36
1		3	4	5	6	7	8	9	10	11											2		37
1		3	4	5	6	7	8*	9	10	11	2†							14			12		38
1		3	4	5	6		8	9	10	11	7*							2			12		39
1		3	4	5	6	7‡	8*	9	10	11				14				2			12		40
1		3	4	5	6	7†	8	9	10*	11				14				2			12		41
1		3	4	5	6	12	8	9†	10	11	14							2			7*		42
42	16	38	40	30	41	35	34	38	41	41	12	29		6	2	3		7			6	1	
	2			1		1			1		11	2	1	8	1	7	2	3	2	2	9	1	
		3	2	2	1	4	11	16	5	7	7	6		1		1		2			3		

1992-93

1	Aug	15	(h)	Wimbledon	W	2-1	Chapman 2	25,795
2		19	(a)	Aston Villa	D	1-1	Speed	29,151
3		22	(a)	Middlesbrough	L	1-4	Cantona	18,649
4		25	(h)	Tottenham H	W	5-0	Rod Wallace, Cantona 3, Chapman	28,218
5		29	(h)	Liverpool	D	2-2	McAllister, Chapman	29,597
6	Sep	1	(a)	Oldham A	D	2-2	Cantona 2	13,848
7		6	(a)	Manchester U	L	0-2		31,296
8		13	(h)	Aston Villa	D	1-1	Hodge	27,815
9		19	(a)	Southampton	D	1-1	Speed	16,229
10		26	(h)	Everton	W	2-0	McAllister, Chapman	27,915
11	Oct	3	(a)	Ipswich T	L	2-4	Chapman, Speed	21,200
12		17	(h)	Sheffield U	W	3-1	Chapman, Speed, Whyte	29,706
13		24	(a)	QPR	L	1-2	Strachan	19,326
14		31	(h)	Coventry C	D	2-2	Chapman, Fairclough	28,018
15	Nov	7	(a)	Manchester C	L	0-4		27,255
16		21	(h)	Arsenal	W	3-0	Fairclough, Chapman, McAllister	30,516
17		29	(a)	Chelsea	L	0-1		24,345
18	Dec	5	(h)	Nottingham F	L	1-4	Speed	29,364
19		12	(h)	Sheffield W	W	3-1	Speed, Chapman, Varadi	29,770
20		20	(a)	Crystal Palace	L	0-1		14,462
21		26	(a)	Blackburn R	L	1-3	McAllister	19,910
22		28	(h)	Norwich C	D	0-0		30,282
23	Jan	9	(h)	Southampton	W	2-1	Chapman, Speed	26,071
24		16	(a)	Everton	L	0-2		21,031
25		30	(h)	Middlesbrough	W	3-0	Strandli, Batty, Fairclough	30,344
26	Feb	6	(a)	Wimbledon	L	0-1		6,704
27		8	(h)	Manchester U	D	0-0		34,166
28		13	(h)	Oldham A	W	2-0	McAllister (pen), Chapman	27,654
29		20	(a)	Tottenham H	L	0-4		32,040
30		24	(a)	Arsenal	D	0-0		21,061
31		27	(h)	Ipswich T	W	1-0	Dorigo	28,848
32	Mar	13	(h)	Manchester C	W	1-0	Rocastle	30,840
33		21	(a)	Nottingham F	D	1-1	Rod Wallace	25,148
34		24	(h)	Chelsea	D	1-1	Wetherall	28,135
35	Apr	6	(a)	Sheffield U	L	1-2	Strandli	20,562
36		10	(h)	Blackburn R	W	5-2	Strachan 3 (1 pen), Rod Wallace, Chapman	31,791
37		14	(a)	Norwich C	L	2-4	Chapman, Rod Wallace	18,613
38		17	(h)	Crystal Palace	D	0-0		27,545
39		21	(a)	Liverpool	L	0-2		34,992
40	May	1	(h)	QPR	D	1-1	Hodge	31,408
41		4	(a)	Sheffield W	D	1-1	Chapman	26,855
42		8	(a)	Coventry C	D	3-3	Rod Wallace 3	19,591

FINAL LEAGUE POSITION: 17th in Premier Division

Appearances

Sub Appearances

Goals

Lukic	Newsome	Dorigo	Batty	Fairclough	Whyte	Cantona	Rod Wallace	Chapman	McAllister	Speed	Hodge	Strachan	Sellars	Wetherall	Shutt	Rocastle	Day	Ray Wallace	Varadi	Sterland	Strandli	Bowman	Kerslake	Forrester	Kerr	Tinkler	Sharp	Whelan	Beeney	
1	2†	3	4*	5	6	7	8	9	10	11	12	14																		1
1	2	3	4*	5	6	7	8	9†	10	11	12	14																		2
1	2†	3	4*	5	6	7	8	9	10	11	12	14																		3
1	2	3	4	5	6	7	8	9	10	11																				4
1	2	3	4*	5†	6	7	8	9	10	11	12	14																		5
1	2	3	4	5	6	7*	8	9	10	11	12																			6
1	2†	3	4	5	6	7	8*	9	10	11	14	12																		7
1	2*		4	5	6	7		9	10	11	12	8	3																	8
1		3	4	5	6			9	10	11	8*	7	12	2†	14															9
1		3	4	5	6	8		9	10	11		7	2*		12															10
1		3	4	5	6	8		9	10	11		7	2*			12														11
1	2	3	4	5	6	8*		9	10	11		7			12															12
1	2	3	4	5	6		8*	9	10†	11		7			12	14														13
1	2	3	4*	5	6	14	8†	9	10	11		7				12														14
	2			5	6	8	9	12	10	11	4*	7		3			1													15
1	2	3		5	6		8*	9	10	11		7			12	4														16
1	2	3		5	6		8	9	10	11		7				4														17
1	2	3		5			8	9	10	11	14	7			12	4†		6*												18
1	2	3		5	6		8*	9	10	11	14	7				4†			12											19
1	2	3		5	6†		8*	9	10	11	14	7				4			12											20
1	12	3	4	5	6			9	10	11		7							8	2*										21
1	12	3	4	5				9	10	11		7		6*					8	2										22
1	14	3		5			4	9	10	11		7*		6	8	12				2†										23
	2*	3	4	12	6		14	9	10	11		7†		5	8		1													24
1		3	4	5	6		9*		10	11		7		2	8†	14					12									25
1	5	3	4		6			9	10	11			2		12	7†					8*									26
1	5	3	4		6			9	10	11	14		2†		8*						12									27
1	5	3	4		6		8	9	10	11	14		2*		12†															28
1	5	3	4		6		8*	9†	10	11	7					12						2								29
1	12	3	4	2	6		8	14	10*	11		7†		5							9									30
1	2	3	4	5			8	12		11		7		6				10			9*									31
1	14	3	4	5†			8	12		11	10			6		7					9*		2							32
1	6	3	4				8†	9		11	10			5		7							2	14						33
1	6	3*	4				8	9†		11	10	12		5		7							2							34
1					6				10†	11	14	7		5									2	8	3	4				35
1	12			5	6		8	9		11		7											2	10*	3	4				36
1	12			5*	6		8	9		11	14	7											2	10†	3	4				37
1	6						8	9	10*	11		7		5									2	4		12	3			38
1	5				6		8	9		11		7			10	4		12					2*				3			39
1	5		4		6		8	9			10					7*		2			14			11†		12	3			40
1	5		4		6		8	9			10							2							12	11	3*	7		41
	5	3	4		6		8	9			10				7*	12		2							14	11†			1	42
39	30	33	30	29	34	12	31	36	32	39	9	25	6	13	6	11	2	5	2	3	4	1	8	5	3	5	4	1	1	
	7			1		1	1	4			14	6	1		8	7		1	2		3			1	2	2				
		1	1	3	1	6	7	15	5	7	2	4		1		1			1		2									

F.A. CUP COMPETITION

1983/84 SEASON

3rd Round
Jan 7 vs Scunthorpe United (h) 1-1
Att: 17,130 Wright

Replay
Jan 10 vs Scunthorpe United (a) 1-1
Att: 13,129 Wright

2nd Replay
Jan 16 vs Scunthorpe United (a) 2-4
Att: 13,312 Wright, Ritchie

1984/85 SEASON

3rd Round
Jan 4 vs Everton (h) 0-2
Att: 21,211

1985/86 SEASON

3rd Round
Jan 4 vs Peterborough United (a) 0-1
Att: 10,137

1986/87 SEASON

3rd Round
Jan 11 vs Telford Town (a) 2-1
Att: 6,460 (at West Brom) Baird 2

4th Round
Feb 3 vs Swindon Town (a) 2-1
Att: 14,031 Quinn (og), Baird

5th Round
Feb 21 vs QPR (h) 2-1
Att: 31,324 Baird, Ormsby

6th Round
Mar 15 vs Wigan Athletic (a) 2-0
Att: 12,479 Stiles, Adams

Semi-Final
April 12 vs Coventry City 2-3 (aet) (90 mins 2-2)
Att: 51,372 (at Hillsborough) Rennie, Edwards

1987/88 SEASON

3rd Round
Jan 9 vs Aston Villa (h) 1-2
Att: 29,002 Davison

1988/89 SEASON

3rd Round
Jan 7 vs Brighton & HA (a) 2-0
Att: 10,900 Baird 2

4th Round
Jan 28 vs Nottingham Forest (a) 0-2
Att: 28,107 Chapman, Parker

1989/90 SEASON

3rd Round
Jan 6 vs Ipswich Town (h) 0-1
Att: 26,766

1990/91 SEASON

3rd Round
Jan 6 vs Barnsley (a) 1-1
Att: 22,424 Sterland

Replay
Jan 9 vs Barnsley (h) 4-0
Att: 19,773 Smith (og), Chapman, McAllister, Strachan (pen)

4th Round
Jan 27 vs Arsenal (a) 0-0
Att: 30,905

Replay
Jan 30 vs Arsenal (h) 1-1 (aet.)
Att: 27,753 Chapman

2nd Replay
Feb 13 vs Arsenal (a) 0-0 (aet.)
Att: 30,433

3rd Replay
Feb 16 vs Arsenal (h) 1-2
Att: 27,190 Chapman

1991/92 SEASON

3rd Round
Jan 15 vs Manchester United (h) 0-1
Att: 31,819

1992/93 SEASON

3rd Round
Jan 2 vs Charlton Athletic (h) 1-1
Att: 21,827 Speed

Replay
Jan 13 vs Charlton Athletic (a) 3-1
Att: 8,337 Speed, Garland (og), McAllister

4th Round
Jan 25 vs Arsenal (a) 2-2
Att: 26,516 Speed, Chapman

Replay
Feb 3 vs Arsenal (h) 2-3 (aet.)
Att: 26,449 Shutt, McAllister

LEAGUE CUP COMPETITION

1983/84 SEASON

2nd Round (1st leg)
Oct 5 vs Chester City (h) 0-1
Att: 8,106

2nd Round (2nd leg)
Oct 26 vs Chester City (a) 4-1 (aggregate 4-2)
Att: 8,044 Ritchie 2, Burns, Barnes

3rd Round
Nov 9 vs Oxford United (h) 1-1
Att: 13,349 McCluskey

Replay
Nov 23 vs Oxford United (a) 1-4
Att: 13,389 Burns

1984/85 SEASON

2nd Round (1st leg)
Sep 25 vs Gillingham (a) 2-1
Att: 8,881 Wright, Ritchie

2nd Round (2nd leg)
Oct 10 vs Gillingham (h) 3-2 (aggregate 5-3)
Att: 11,109 Gavin, Sellars, Ritchie

3rd Round
Oct 31 vs Watford (h) 0-4
Att: 21,221

1985/86 SEASON

2nd Round (1st leg)
Sep 25 vs Walsall (h) 0-0
Att: 8,869

2nd Round (2nd leg)
Oct 7 vs Walsall (a) 3-0 (aggregate 3-0)
Att: 7,085 Linighan, Snodin 2

3rd Round
Oct 30 vs Aston Villa (h) 0-3
Att: 15,444

1986/87 SEASON

2nd Round (1st leg)
Sep 23 vs Oldham Athletic (a) 2-3
Att: 5,569 Aspin, Taylor

2nd Round (2nd leg)
Oct 8 vs Oldham Athletic (h) 0-1 (aggregate 2-4)
Att: 11,449

1987/88 SEASON

2nd Round (1st leg)
Sep 23 vs York City (h) 1-1
Att: 11,527 Snodin

2nd Round (2nd leg)
Oct 6 vs York City (a) 4-0 (aggregate 5-1)
Att: 5,996 Sheridan 2, Taylor, Mumby

3rd Round
Oct 28 vs Oldham Athletic (h) 2-2
Att: 15,600 Swan 2

Replay
Nov 4 vs Oldham Athletic (a) 2-4
Att: 7,058 Snodin, Taylor

1988/89 SEASON

2nd Round (1st leg)
Sep 27 vs Peterborough United (a) 2-1
Att: 4,979 Pearson, Baird

2nd Round (2nd leg)
Oct 12 vs Peterborough United (h) 3-1 (agg. 5-2)
Att: 8,894 Davison, Hilaire, Sheridan (pen)

3rd Round
Nov 2 vs Luton Town (h) 0-2
Att: 19,447

1989/90 SEASON

2nd Round (1st leg)
Sep 19 vs Oldham Athletic (a) 1-2
Att: 8,415 Strachan

2nd Round (2nd leg)
Oct 3 vs Oldham Athletic (h) 1-2 (aggregate 2-4)
Att: 18,092 Fairclough

1990/91 SEASON

2nd Round (1st leg)
Sep 26 vs Leicester City (a) 0-1
Att: 13,744

2nd Round (2nd leg)
Oct 10 vs Leicester City (h) 3-0 (aggregate 3-1)
Att: 19,090 Walsh (og), Speed, Strachan

3rd Round
Oct 31 vs Oldham Athletic (h) 2-0
Att: 26,327 Chapman, Speed

4th Round
Nov 27 vs QPR (a) 3-0
Att: 15,832 McAllister, Fairclough, Chapman

5th Round
Jan 16 vs Aston Villa (h) 4-1
Att: 28,176 Chapman 2, McAllister, Speed

Semi-Final (1st leg)
Feb 10 vs Manchester United (a) 1-2
Att: 34,050 Whyte

Semi-Final (2nd leg)
Feb 24 vs Manchester United (h) 0-1 (agg. 1-3)
Att: 32,014

1991/92 SEASON

2nd Round (1st leg)
Sep 24 vs Scunthorpe United (a) 0-0
Att: 8,392

2nd Round (2nd leg)
Oct 8 vs Scunthorpe United (h) 3-0 (agg. 3-0)
Att: 14,558 Sterland (pen), Chapman, Speed

3rd Round
Oct 29 vs Tranmere Rovers (h) 3-1
Att: 18,266 Chapman 2, Shutt

4th Round
Dec 4 vs Everton (a) 4-1
Att: 25,467 Speed, Chapman, Wallace 2

5th Round
Jan 8 vs Manchester United (h) 1-3
Att: 28,886 Speed

1992/93 SEASON

2nd Round (1st leg)
Sep 22 vs Scunthorpe United (h) 4-1
Att: 10,113 Strachan, Chapman, Speed, Shutt

2nd Round (2nd leg)
Oct 27 vs Scunthorpe United (a) 0-0 (agg. 4-1)
Att: 7,419

3rd Round
Nov 10 vs Watford (a) 1-2
Att: 18,035 McAllister

1983-84 SEASON

SECOND DIVISION

Chelsea	42	25	13	4	90	40	89
Sheffield Wednesday	42	26	10	6	72	34	89
Newcastle United	42	24	8	10	85	53	80
Manchester City	42	20	10	12	66	48	70
Grimsby Town	42	19	13	10	60	47	70
Blackburn Rovers	42	17	16	9	57	46	67
Carlisle United	42	16	16	10	48	41	64
Shrewsbury Town	42	17	10	15	49	53	61
Brighton & Hove Alb.	42	17	9	16	69	60	60
Leeds United	**42**	**16**	**12**	**14**	**55**	**56**	**60**
Fulham	42	15	12	15	60	53	57
Huddersfield Town	42	14	15	13	56	49	57
Charlton Athletic	42	16	9	17	53	64	57
Barnsley	42	15	7	20	57	53	52
Cardiff City	42	15	6	21	53	66	51
Portsmouth	42	14	7	21	73	64	49
Middlesbrough	42	12	13	17	41	47	49
Crystal Palace	42	12	11	19	42	52	47
Oldham Athletic	42	13	8	21	47	73	47
Derby County	42	11	9	22	36	72	42
Swansea City	42	7	8	27	36	85	29
Cambridge United	42	4	12	26	28	77	24

1984-85 SEASON

SECOND DIVISION

Oxford United	42	25	9	8	84	36	84
Birmingham City	42	25	7	10	59	33	82
Manchester City	42	21	11	10	66	40	74
Portsmouth	42	20	14	8	69	50	74
Blackburn Rovers	42	21	10	11	66	41	73
Brighton & Hove Alb.	42	20	12	10	58	34	72
Leeds United	**42**	**19**	**12**	**11**	**66**	**43**	**69**
Shrewsbury Town	42	18	11	13	66	53	65
Fulham	42	19	8	15	68	64	65
Grimsby Town	42	18	8	16	72	64	62
Barnsley	42	14	16	12	42	42	58
Wimbledon	42	16	10	16	71	75	58
Huddersfield Town	42	15	10	17	52	64	55
Oldham Athletic	42	15	8	19	49	67	53
Crystal Palace	42	12	12	18	46	65	48
Carlisle United	42	13	8	21	50	67	47
Charlton Athletic	42	11	12	19	51	63	45
Sheffield United	42	10	14	18	54	66	44
Middlesbrough	42	10	10	22	41	57	40
Notts County	42	10	7	25	45	73	37
Cardiff	42	9	8	25	47	79	35
Wolves	42	8	9	25	37	79	33

1985-86 SEASON

SECOND DIVISION

Norwich City	42	25	9	8	84	39	84
Charlton Athletic	42	22	11	9	78	45	77
Wimbledon	42	21	13	8	58	37	76
Portsmouth	42	22	7	13	69	41	73
Crystal Palace	42	19	9	14	57	52	66
Hull City	42	17	13	12	65	55	64
Sheffield United	42	17	11	14	64	63	62
Oldham Athletic	42	17	9	16	62	61	60
Millwall	42	17	8	17	64	65	59
Stoke City	42	14	15	13	48	50	57
Brighton & Hove Alb.	42	16	8	18	64	64	56
Barnsley	42	14	14	14	47	50	56
Bradford City	42	16	6	20	51	63	54
Leeds United	**42**	**15**	**8**	**19**	**56**	**72**	**53**
Grimsby Town	42	14	10	18	58	62	52
Huddersfield Town	42	14	10	18	51	67	52
Shrewsbury Town	42	14	9	19	52	64	51
Sunderland	42	13	11	18	47	61	50
Blackburn Rovers	42	12	13	17	53	62	49
Carlisle United	42	13	7	22	47	71	46
Middlesbrough	42	12	9	21	44	53	45
Fulham	42	10	6	26	45	69	36

1986-87 SEASON

SECOND DIVISION

Derby County	42	25	9	8	64	38	84
Portsmouth	42	23	9	10	53	28	78
Oldham Athletic	42	22	9	11	65	44	75
Leeds United	**42**	**19**	**11**	**12**	**58**	**44**	**68**
Ipswich Town	42	17	13	12	59	43	64
Crystal Palace	42	19	5	18	51	53	62
Plymouth Argyle	42	16	13	13	62	57	61
Stoke City	42	16	10	16	63	53	58
Sheffield United	42	15	13	14	50	49	58
Bradford City	42	15	10	17	62	62	55
Barnsley	42	14	13	15	49	52	55
Blackburn Rovers	42	15	10	17	45	55	55
Reading	42	14	11	17	52	59	53
Hull City	42	13	14	15	41	55	53
West Brom	42	13	12	17	51	49	51
Millwall	42	14	9	19	39	45	51
Huddersfield Town	42	13	12	17	54	61	51
Shrewsbury Town	42	15	6	21	41	63	51
Birmingham City	42	11	17	14	47	59	50
Sunderland	42	12	12	18	49	59	48
Grimsby Town	42	10	14	18	39	59	44
Brighton & Hove Alb.	42	9	12	21	37	54	39

1987-88 SEASON

SECOND DIVISION

Millwall	44	25	7	12	72	52	82
Aston Villa	44	22	12	10	68	41	78
Middlesbrough	44	22	12	10	63	36	78
Bradford City	44	22	11	11	74	54	77
Blackburn Rovers	44	21	14	9	68	52	77
Crystal Palace	44	22	9	13	86	59	75
Leeds United	**44**	**19**	**12**	**13**	**61**	**51**	**69**
Ipswich Town	44	19	9	16	61	52	66
Manchester City	44	19	8	17	80	60	65
Oldham Athletic	44	18	11	15	72	64	65
Stoke City	44	17	11	16	50	57	62
Swindon Town	44	16	11	17	73	60	59
Leicester City	44	16	11	17	62	61	59
Barnsley	44	15	12	17	61	62	57
Hull City	44	14	15	15	54	60	57
Plymouth Argyle	44	16	8	20	65	67	56
Bournemouth	44	13	10	21	56	68	49
Shrewsbury Town	44	11	16	17	42	54	49
Birmingham City	44	11	15	18	41	66	48
West Brom	44	12	11	21	50	69	47
Sheffield United	44	13	7	24	45	74	46
Reading	44	10	12	22	44	70	42
Huddersfield Town	44	6	10	28	41	100	28

1988-89 SEASON

SECOND DIVISION

Chelsea	46	29	12	5	96	50	99
Manchester City	46	23	13	10	77	53	82
Crystal Palace	46	23	12	11	71	49	81
Watford	46	22	12	12	74	48	78
Blackburn Rovers	46	22	11	13	74	59	77
Swindon Town	46	20	16	10	68	53	76
Barnsley	46	20	14	12	66	58	74
Ipswich Town	46	22	7	17	71	61	73
West Brom	46	18	18	10	65	41	72
Leeds United	**46**	**17**	**16**	**13**	**59**	**50**	**67**
Sunderland	46	16	15	15	60	60	63
Bournemouth	46	18	8	20	53	62	62
Stoke City	46	15	14	17	57	72	59
Bradford City	46	13	17	16	52	59	56
Leicester City	46	13	16	17	56	63	55
Oldham Athletic	46	11	21	14	75	72	54
Oxford United	46	14	12	20	62	70	54
Plymouth Argyle	46	14	12	20	55	66	54
Brighton & Hove Alb.	46	14	9	23	57	66	51
Portsmouth	46	13	12	21	53	62	51
Hull City	46	11	14	21	52	68	47
Shrewsbury Town	46	8	18	20	40	67	42
Birmingham City	46	8	11	27	31	76	35
Walsall	46	5	16	25	41	80	31

1988-90 SEASON

SECOND DIVISION

Leeds United	**46**	**24**	**13**	**9**	**79**	**52**	**85**
Sheffield United	46	24	13	9	78	58	85
Newcastle United	46	22	14	10	80	55	80
Swindon Town	46	20	14	12	79	59	74
Blackburn Rovers	46	19	17	10	74	59	74
Sunderland	46	20	14	12	70	64	74
West Ham United	46	20	12	14	80	57	72
Oldham Athletic	46	19	14	13	70	57	71
Ipswich Town	46	19	12	15	67	66	69
Wolves	46	18	13	15	67	60	67
Port Vale	46	15	16	15	62	57	61
Portsmouth	46	15	16	15	62	65	61
Leicester City	46	15	14	17	67	79	59
Hull City	46	14	16	16	58	65	58
Watford	46	14	15	17	58	60	57
Plymouth Argyle	46	14	13	19	58	63	55
Oxford United	46	15	9	22	57	66	54
Brighton & Hove Alb.	46	15	9	22	56	72	54
Barnsley	46	13	15	18	49	71	54
West Brom	46	12	15	19	67	71	51
Middlesbrough	46	13	11	22	52	63	50
Bournemouth	46	12	12	22	57	76	48
Bradford City	46	9	14	23	44	68	41
Stoke City	46	6	19	21	35	63	37

1990-91 SEASON

FIRST DIVISION

Arsenal	38	24	13	1	74	18	83
Liverpool	38	23	7	8	77	40	76
Crystal Palace	38	20	9	9	50	41	69
Leeds United	**38**	**19**	**7**	**12**	**65**	**47**	**64**
Manchester City	38	17	11	10	64	53	62
Manchester United	38	16	12	10	58	45	59
Wimbledon	38	14	14	10	53	46	56
Nottingham Forest	38	14	12	12	65	50	54
Everton	38	13	12	13	50	46	51
Tottenham	38	11	16	11	51	50	49
Chelsea	38	13	10	15	58	69	49
QPR	38	12	10	16	44	53	46
Sheffield United	38	13	7	18	36	55	46
Southampton	38	12	9	17	58	69	45
Norwich City	38	13	6	19	41	64	45
Coventry City	38	11	11	16	42	49	44
Aston Villa	38	9	14	15	46	58	41
Luton Town	38	10	7	21	42	61	37
Sunderland	38	8	10	20	38	60	34
Derby County	38	5	9	24	37	75	24

Arsenal 2 points deducted
Manchester United 1 point deducted

1991-92 SEASON

FIRST DIVISION

Leeds United	**42**	**22**	**16**	**4**	**74**	**37**	**82**
Manchester United	42	21	15	6	63	33	78
Sheffield Wednesday	42	21	12	9	62	49	75
Arsenal	42	19	15	8	81	46	72
Manchester City	42	20	10	12	61	48	70
Liverpool	42	16	16	10	47	40	64
Aston Villa	42	17	9	16	48	44	60
Nottingham Forest	42	16	11	15	60	58	59
Sheffield United	42	16	9	17	65	63	57
Crystal Palace	42	14	15	13	53	61	57
QPR	42	12	18	12	48	47	54
Everton	42	13	14	15	52	51	53
Wimbledon	42	13	14	15	53	53	53
Chelsea	42	13	14	15	50	60	53
Tottenham	42	15	7	20	58	63	52
Southampton	42	14	10	18	39	55	52
Oldham Athletic	42	14	9	19	63	67	51
Norwich City	42	11	12	19	47	63	45
Coventry City	42	11	11	20	35	44	44
Luton Town	42	10	12	20	38	71	42
Notts County	42	10	10	22	40	62	40
West Ham United	42	9	11	22	37	59	38

1992-93 SEASON

PREMIER DIVISION

Manchester United	42	24	12	6	67	31	84
Aston Villa	42	21	11	10	57	40	74
Norwich City	42	21	9	12	61	65	72
Blackburn Rovers	42	20	11	11	68	46	71
QPR	42	17	12	13	63	55	63
Liverpool	42	16	11	15	62	55	59
Sheffield Wednesday	42	15	14	13	55	51	59
Tottenham	42	16	11	15	60	66	59
Manchester City	42	15	12	15	56	51	57
Arsenal	42	15	11	16	40	38	56
Chelsea	42	14	14	14	51	54	56
Wimbledon	42	14	12	16	56	55	54
Everton	42	15	8	19	53	55	53
Sheffield United	42	14	10	18	54	53	52
Coventry City	42	13	13	16	52	57	52
Ipswich Town	42	12	16	14	50	55	52
Leeds United	**42**	**12**	**15**	**15**	**57**	**62**	**51**
Southampton	42	13	11	18	54	61	50
Oldham Athletic	42	13	10	19	63	74	49
Crystal Palace	42	11	16	15	48	61	49
Middlesbrough	42	11	11	20	54	75	44
Nottingham Forest	42	10	10	22	41	62	40

Vinny Jones

Played an important role in the 1989-90 promotion season before moving on to Sheffield United

ADAMS, Michael R.

Sheffield, 8th November 1961

Source	Season	Club	Apps.	Gls
App	1979-80	Gillingham	4	-
	1980-81		13	-
	1981-82		31	2
	1982-83		44	3
Tr	1983-84	Coventry C	17	1
	1984-85		31	3
	1985-86		31	3
	1986-87		11	2
Tr	1986-87	Leeds U	17	1
	1987-88		40	-
	1988-89		16	1
Tr	1988-89	Southampton	8	-
	1989-90		15	-
	1990-91		30	-
	1991-92		34	3
	1992-93		38	4

AGANA, P. Anthony

Bromley, 2nd October 1963

Source	Season	Club	Apps.	Gls
From Weymouth				
	1987-88	Watford	15	1
Tr	1987-88	Sheffield U	12	2
	1988-89		46	24
	1989-90		31	10
	1990-91		16	2
	1991-92		13	4
Tr	1991-92	Notts Co	13	1
L	1991-92	Leeds U	2	-
	1992-93	Notts Co	29	2

AIZLEWOOD, Mark

Newport, 1st October 1959

Source	Season	Club	Apps.	Gls
App	1975-76	Newport Co	6	-
	1976-77		5	-
	1977-78		27	1
Tr	1977-78	Luton T	-	-
	1978-79		39	-
	1979-80		10	-
	1980-81		23	-
	1981-82		26	3
Tr	1982-83	Charlton A	22	1
	1983-84		31	1
	1984-85		38	3
	1985-86		35	3
	1986-87		26	1
Tr	1986-87	Leeds U	15	-
	1987-88		17	-
	1988-89		38	3
Tr	1989-90	Bradford C	39	1
Tr	1990-91	Bristol C	42	2
	1991-92		34	1
	1992-93		20	-

ANDREWS, Ian E.

Nottingham, 1st December 1964

Source	Season	Club	Apps.	Gls
App	1983-84	Leicester C	2	-
L	1983-84	Swindon T	1	-
	1984-85	Leicester C	31	-
	1985-86		39	-
	1986-87		42	-
	1987-88		12	-
Tr	1988-89	Glasgow Celtic	5	-
L	1988-89	Leeds U	1	-
Tr	1989-90	Southampton	3	-
	1990-91		1	-
	1991-92		1	-
	1992-93		-	-

ASHURST, John (Jack)

Coatbridge, 12th October 1954

Source	Season	Club	Apps.	Gls
App	1972-73	Sunderland	11	-
	1973-74		19	1
	1974-75		6	-
	1975-76		21	-
	1976-77		31	-
	1977-78		38	2
	1978-79		11	1
	1979-80		3	-
Tr	1979-80	Blackpool	25	-
	1980-81		28	3
Tr	1981-82	Carlisle U	46	1
	1982-83		30	-
	1983-84		41	1
	1984-85		42	-
	1985-86		35	-
Tr	1986-87	Leeds U	41	1
	1987-88		41	-
	1988-89		7	-
Tr	1988-89	Doncaster R	30	1
	1989-90		43	-
From Bridlington Town				
	1990-91	Doncaster R	29	1
	1991-92		37	-
Tr	1992-93	Rochdale	1	-

ASPIN, Neil

Gateshead, 12th April 1965

Source	Season	Club	Apps.	Gls
App	1981-82	Leeds U	1	-
	1982-83		15	-
	1983-84		21	1
	1984-85		32	1
	1985-86		38	2
	1986-87		41	1
	1987-88		26	
	1988-89		33	-
Tr	1989-90	Port Vale	42	-
	1990-91		41	1
	1991-92		42	-
	1992-93		35	-

BAIRD, Ian J.

Rotherham, 1st April 1964

Source	Season	Club	Apps.	Gls
App	1982-83	Southampton	11	2
	1983-84		6	1

Source	Season	Club	Apps.	Gls
L	1983-84	Cardiff C	12	6
	1984-85	Southampton	5	2
L	1984-85	Newcastle U	5	1
Tr	1984-85	Leeds U	10	6
	1985-86		35	12
	1986-87		40	15
Tr	1987-88	Portsmouth	20	1
Tr	1987-88	Leeds U	10	3
	1988-89		43	10
	1989-90		24	4
Tr	1989-90	Middlesbrough	19	5
	1990-91		44	14
Tr	1991-93	Heart of Midlothian	64	15

BARNES, Peter S.

Manchester, 10th June 1957

Source	Season	Club	Apps.	Gls
App	1974-75	Manchester C	3	1
	1975-76		28	3
	1976-77		21	2
	1977-78		34	8
	1978-79		29	1
Tr	1979-80	West Brom A	38	15
	1980-81		39	8
Tr	1981-82	Leeds U	30	1
From Real Betis (Spain)				
	1983-84	Leeds U	27	4
Tr	1984-85	Coventry C	18	2
Tr	1985-86	Manchester U	13	2
	1986-87		7	-
Tr	1986-87	Manchester C	8	-
Tr	1987-88	Hull C	11	-
Tr	1987-88	Manchester C	-	-
L	1987-88	Bolton W	2	-
L	1987-88	Port Vale	3	-
Tr	1988-89	Bolton W	3	-
Tr	1988-89	Sunderland	1	-

BATTY, David

Leeds, 2nd December 1968

Source	Season	Club	Apps.	Gls
YT	1987-88	Leeds U	23	1
	1988-89		30	-
	1989-90		42	-
	1990-91		37	-
	1991-92		40	2
	1992-93		30	1

BEENEY, Mark

Pembury, 30th December 1967

Source	Season	Club	Apps.	Gls
	1986-87	Gillingham	2	-
Tr	1987-88	Maidstone U	-	-
	1988-89		-	-
	1989-90		33	-
L	1989-90	Aldershot	7	-
	1990-91	Maidstone U	17	-
Tr	1990-91	Brighton & HA	2	-
	1991-92		25	-
	1992-93		42	-
Tr	1992-93	Leeds U	1	-

David Batty
Popular, Leeds-born international midfielder

BEGLIN, James M.

Waterford, 19th July 1963

Source	Season	Club	Apps.	Gls
From Shamrock Rovers				
	1984-85	Liverpool	10	1
	1985-86		34	1
	1986-87		20	-
Tr	1989-90	Leeds U	19	-
L	1989-90	Plymouth A	5	-
L	1990-91	Blackburn R	6	-

BLAKE, Noel L. G.

Jamaica, 12th January 1962

Source	Season	Club	Apps.	Gls
From Sutton Coldfield Town				
	1979-80	Aston Villa	3	-
	1981-82		1	-
L	1981-82	Shrewsbury T	6	-
Tr	1982-83	Birmingham C	37	3
	1983-84		39	2
Tr	1984-85	Portsmouth	42	3
	1985-86		42	4
	1986-87		41	3
	1987-88		19	-
Tr	1988-89	Leeds U	44	4
	1989-90		7	-
Tr	1989-90	Stoke C	18	-
	1990-91		44	3
	1991-92		13	-
L	1991-92	Bradford C	6	-
Tr	1992-93	Bradford C	32	3

Source	Season	Club	Apps.	Gls

BOWMAN, Robert

Durham, 21st November 1975

Source	Season	Club	Apps.	Gls
YT	1992-93	Leeds U	4	-

BROCKIE, Vincent

Greenock, 2nd February 1969

Source	Season	Club	Apps.	Gls
YT	1987-88	Leeds U	2	-
Tr	1988-89	Doncaster R	23	2
	1989-90		24	3
	1990-91		7	2

BROWN, Anthony J.

Bradford, 17th September 1958

From Thackley

Source	Season	Club	Apps.	Gls
	1982-83	Leeds U	1	-
	1983-84		22	1
	1984-85		1	-
L	1984-85	Doncaster R	14	-
Tr	1985-86	Doncaster R	38	2
	1986-87		35	-
Tr	1987-88	Scunthorpe U	22	-
	1988-89		32	2
Tr	1989-90	Rochdale	43	-
	1990-91		26	-
	1991-92		40	-
	1992-93		5	-

BUCKLEY, John W.

Glasgow, 10th May 1962

From Queen's Park and Celtic

Source	Season	Club	Apps.	Gls
	1982-84	Partick T	45	5
Tr	1984-85	Doncaster R	39	6
	1985-86		45	5
Tr	1986-87	Leeds U	9	1
L	1986-87	Leicester C	5	-
	1987-88	Leeds U	1	-
L	1987-88	Doncaster R	6	-
Tr	1987-88	Rotherham U	26	-
	1988-89		36	5
	1989-90		40	7
	1990-91		3	1
Tr	1990-91	Partick T	26	5
Tr	1991-92	Scunthorpe U	28	6
	1992-93		15	2
Tr	1992-93	Rotherham U	4	-

BURNS, Kenneth

Glasgow, 23rd September 1953

Source	Season	Club	Apps.	Gls
App	1971-72	Birmingham C	8	-
	1972-73		14	3
	1973-74		37	10
	1974-75		39	8
	1975-76		36	5
	1976-77		36	19
Tr	1977-78	Nottingham F	41	4
	1978-79		25	-
	1979-80		34	3
	1980-81		30	5
	1981-82		7	1
Tr	1981-82	Leeds U	23	-
	1982-83		20	2
L	1982-83	Derby Co	7	1
	1983-84	Leeds U	13	-
Tr	1983-84	Derby Co	11	-
	1984-85		20	1
L	1984-85	Notts Co	2	-
Tr	1985-86	Barnsley	22	-

BUTTERWORTH, Aidan J.

Leeds, 7th November 1961

Source	Season	Club	Apps.	Gls
Jnrs	1980-81	Leeds U	1	-
	1981-82		14	3
	1982-83		38	11
	1983-84		11	1
Tr	1984-85	Doncaster R	29	5
	1985-86		21	-

CANTONA, Eric

Paris, 24th May 1966

From Nimes (France)

Source	Season	Club	Apps.	Gls
	1991-92	Leeds U	15	3
	1992-93		13	6
Tr	1992-93	Manchester U	22	9

CASWELL, Brian L.

Wednesbury, 14th February 1956

Source	Season	Club	Apps.	Gls
App	1972-73	Walsall	4	-
	1973-74		15	-
	1974-75		22	1
	1975-76		17	-
	1976-77		38	2
	1977-78		36	3
	1978-79		42	1
	1979-80		45	6
	1980-81		34	1
	1981-82		41	3
	1982-83		39	-
	1983-84		32	-
	1984-85		35	-
Tr	1985-86	Doncaster R	15	2
Tr	1985-86	Leeds U	8	-

CHAPMAN, Lee R.

Lincoln, 5th December 1959

From Stoke City Juniors

Source	Season	Club	Apps.	Gls
L	1978-79	Plymouth A	4	-
	1979-80	Stoke C	17	3
	1980-81		41	15
	1981-82	Stoke C	41	16
Tr	1982-83	Arsenal	19	3
	1983-84		4	1
Tr	1983-84	Sunderland	15	3
Tr	1984-85	Sheffield W	40	15

Source	Season	Club	Apps.	Gls

Lee Chapman

Prolific goalscorer for Leeds

Source	Season	Club	Apps.	Gls
	1985-86		31	10
	1986-87		41	19
	1987-88		37	19
Tr	1988-89	Nottingham F	30	8
	1989-90		18	7
Niort	1989-90	Leeds U	21	12
	1990-91		38	21
	1991-92		38	16
	1992-93		40	14

DAVISON, Robert

South Shields, 17th July 1959

Source	Season	Club	Apps.	Gls
From Seaham C.W.				
	1980-81	Huddersfield T	2	-
Tr	1981-82	Halifax T	46	20
	1982-83		17	9
Tr	1982-83	Derby Co	26	8
	1983-84		40	14
	1984-85		46	24
	1985-86		41	17
	1986-87		40	19
	1987-88		13	1
Tr	1987-88	Leeds U	16	5
	1988-89		39	14
	1989-90		29	11
	1990-91		5	1
	1991-92		2	-
L	1991-92	Derby Co	10	8
L	1991-92	Sheffield U	11	4
Tr	1992-93	Leicester C	25	6

DAY, Mervyn R.

Chelmsford, 26th June 1955

Source	Season	Club	Apps.	Gls
App	1973-74	West Ham U	33	-
	1974-75		42	-
	1975-76		41	-
	1976-77		42	-
	1977-78		23	-
	1978-79		13	-
Tr	1979-80	Orient	42	-
	1980-81		40	-
	1981-82		42	-
	1982-83		46	-
Tr	1983-84	Aston Villa	14	-
	1984-85		16	-
Tr	1984-85	Leeds U	18	-
	1985-86		40	-
	1986-87		34	-
	1987-88		44	-
	1988-89		45	-
	1989-90		44	-
	1990-91		-	-
L	1990-91	Coventry C	-	-
	1991-92	Leeds U	-	-
L	1991-92	Luton T	4	-
L	1991-92	Sheffield U	1	-
	1992-93	Leeds U	2	-

DE MANGE, Kenneth J. P.

Dublin, 3rd September 1964

Source	Season	Club	Apps.	Gls
From Home Farm				
	1983-87	Liverpool	-	-
L	1986-87	Scunthorpe U	3	2
	1987-88	Liverpool	-	-
Tr	1987-88	Leeds U	15	1
Tr	1987-88	Hull C	9	1
	1988-89		32	1
	1989-90		21	-
	1990-91		6	-
L	1990-91	Cardiff C	15	-
	1991-92	Hull C	-	-

DICKINSON, Martin J.

Leeds, 14th March 1963

Source	Season	Club	Apps.	Gls
App	1979-80	Leeds U	6	-
	1980-81		1	-
	1982-83		31	-
	1983-84		34	-
	1984-85		12	1
	1985-86		19	1
Tr	1985-86	West Brom A	7	-

Source	Season	Club	Apps.	Gls
	1986-87	West Brom A	27	1
	1987-88		16	1
Tr	1988-89	Sheffield U	1	-

DOIG, Russell

Millport, 17th January 1964

Source	Season	Club	Apps.	Gls
From St.Mirren				
	1983-86	East Stirling	109	9
Tr	1986-87	Leeds U	4	-
L	1986-87	Peterborough U	7	-
Tr	1987-88	Hartlepool U	9	-
	1988-89		19	1
	1989-90		5	-

DONNELLY, John

Glasgow, 8th March 1961

Source	Season	Club	Apps.	Gls
From Apprentice, Notts County				
	1978-80	Motherwell	19	2
Tr	1980-83	Dumbarton	78	17
Tr	1982-83	Leeds U	14	1
	1983-84		25	3

DORIGO, Anthony R.

Melbourne (Australia), 31st December 1965

Source	Season	Club	Apps.	Gls
App	1983-84	Aston Villa	1	-
	1984-85		31	-
	1985-86		38	1
	1986-87		41	-
Tr	1987-88	Chelsea	40	-
	1988-89		40	6
	1989-90		35	3
	1990-91		31	2
Tr	1991-92	Leeds U	38	3
	1992-93		33	1

EDWARDS, Keith

Stockton, 16th July 1957

Source	Season	Club	Apps.	Gls
Jnrs	1975-76	Sheffield U	3	-
	1976-77		31	18
	1977-78		36	11
Tr	1978-79	Hull C	46	24
	1979-80		41	19
	1980-81		40	13
	1981-82		5	1
Tr	1981-82	Sheffield U	41	35
	1982-83		42	13
	1983-84		44	33
	1984-85		29	13
	1985-86		35	20
Tr	1986-87	Leeds U	30	6
	1987-88		8	-
Tr	1987-88	Aberdeen	9	2
Tr	1987-88	Hull C	9	3
	1988-89		44	26
	1989-90		2	-
Tr	1989-90	Stockport Co	27	10
L	1989-90	Huddersfield T	10	4
Tr	1990-91	Huddersfield T	18	4
L	1990-91	Plymouth A	3	1

ELI, Roger

Bradford, 11th September 1965

Source	Season	Club	Apps.	Gls
App	1984-85	Leeds U	1	-
	1985-86		1	-
Tr	1985-86	Wolverhampton W	14	-
	1986-87		4	-
Tr	1987-88	Cambridge U	-	-
Tr	1987-88	Crewe Alex	27	1
Tr	1988-89	York C	4	1
Tr	1988-89	Bury	2	-
From Northwich Victoria				
	1989-90	Burnley	29	-
	1990-91		26	1
	1991-92		33	10
	1992-93		11	-

FAIRCLOUGH, Courtney H. (Chris)

Nottingham, 12th April 1964

Source	Season	Club	Apps.	Gls
App	1982-83	Nottingham F	15	-
	1983-84		31	-
	1984-85		35	-
	1986-87		26	1
Tr	1987-88	Tottenham H	40	4
	1988-89		20	1
Tr	1988-89	Leeds U	11	-
	1989-90		42	8
	1990-91		34	4
	1991-92		31	2
	1992-93		30	3

FORRESTER, Jamie

Bradford, 1st November 1974

Source	Season	Club	Apps.	Gls
From Auxerre				
	1992-93	Leeds U	6	-

GAVIN, Mark W.

Baillieston, 10th December 1963

Source	Season	Club	Apps.	Gls
App	1982-83	Leeds U	7	1
	1983-84		12	1
	1984-85		11	1
L	1984-85	Hartlepool U	7	-
Tr	1985-86	Carlisle U	13	1
Tr	1985-86	Bolton W	8	1
	1986-87		41	2
Tr	1987-88	Rochdale	23	6
Tr	1987-89	Heart of Midlothian	9	-
Tr	1988-89	Bristol C	29	3
	1989-90		40	3
Tr	1990-91	Watford	13	-
Tr	1991-92	Bristol C	14	1
	1992-93		19	1

Source	Season	Club	Apps.	Gls

GRAY, Edward

Glasgow, 17th January 1948

Source	Season	Club	Apps.	Gls
	1965-66	Leeds U	3	1
	1966-67		29	4
	1967-68		32	6
	1968-69		33	5
	1969-70		30	9
	1970-71		19	1
	1971-72		26	6
	1972-73		17	1
	1973-74		8	-
	1974-75		12	1
	1975-76		29	1
	1976-77		37	5
	1977-78		27	5
	1978-79		28	4
	1979-80		30	2
	1980-81		38	-
	1981-82		29	1
	1982-83		21	-
	1983-84		4	-

GRAY, Frank T.

Glasgow, 27th October 1954

Source	Season	Club	Apps.	Gls
App	1972-73	Leeds U	4	1
	1973-74		6	-
	1974-75		18	2
	1975-76		42	2
	1976-77		41	3
	1977-78		41	3
	1978-79		41	6
Tr	1979-80	Nottingham F	41	2
	1980-81		40	3
Tr	1981-82	Leeds U	37	-
	1982-83		42	5
	1983-84		24	4
	1984-85		39	1
Tr	1985-86	Sunderland	34	4
	1986-87		38	4
	1987-88		34	-
	1988-89		40	-
Tr	1989-90	Darlington	36	1
	1990-91		43	7
	1991-92		6	-

GRAYSON, Simon N. K.

Ripon, 16th December 1969

Source	Season	Club	Apps.	Gls
YT	1987-88	Leeds U	2	-
Tr	1991-92	Leicester C	13	-
	1992-93		24	1

HADDOCK, Peter M.

Newcastle, 9th December 1961

Source	Season	Club	Apps.	Gls
App	1981-82	Newcastle U	30	-
	1982-83		17	-
	1983-84		3	-
	1984-85		1	-
	1985-86		6	-
L	1985-86	Burnley	7	-
Tr	1986-87	Leeds U	11	-
	1987-88		40	1
	1988-89		12	-
	1989-90		40	-
	1990-91		15	-

HAMSON, Gary

Nottingham, 24th August 1959

Source	Season	Club	Apps.	Gls
App	1976-77	Sheffield U	29	1
	1977-78		38	3
	1978-79		41	4
Tr	1979-80	Leeds U	19	1
	1980-81		11	-
	1981-82		18	2
	1983-84		25	-
	1984-85		31	-
	1985-86		30	-

HARLE, David

Denaby, 15th August 1963

Source	Season	Club	Apps.	Gls
App	1979-80	Doncaster R	1	-
	1980-81		34	1
	1981-82		26	2
Tr	1982-83	Exeter C	37	6
	1983-84		6	-
Tr	1983-84	Doncaster R	29	6
	1984-85		37	9
	1985-86		17	2
Tr	1985-86	Leeds U	3	-
L	1985-86	Bristol C	8	-
Tr	1986-87	Bristol C	15	2
Tr	1986-87	Scunthorpe U	26	2
	1987-88		45	6
	1988-89		18	2
Tr	1988-89	Peterborough U	7	-
	1989-90		15	2
Tr	1989-90	Doncaster R	10	-
	1990-91		22	2
	1991-92		13	1

HARVEY, David

Leeds, 7th February 1948

Source	Season	Club	Apps.	Gls
Jnrs	1965-66	Leeds U	2	-
	1966-67		3	-
	1967-68		6	-
	1969-70		5	-
	1970-71		7	-
	1971-72		7	-
	1972-73		41	-
	1973-74		39	-
	1974-75		27	-
	1975-76		40	-
	1976-77		26	-
	1977-78		25	-
	1978-79		39	-
	1979-80		9	-

From Vancouver Whitecaps

Source	Season	Club	Apps.	Gls
	1980-81	Leeds U	-	-
From Vancouver Whitecaps				
	1982-83	Leeds U	13	-
	1983-84		40	-

HENDRIE, John G.

Lennoxtown, 24th October 1963

Source	Season	Club	Apps.	Gls
App	1981-82	Coventry C	6	-
	1982-83		12	2
	1983-84		3	-
L	1983-84	Hereford U	6	-
Tr	1984-85	Bradford C	46	9
	1985-86		42	10
	1986-87		42	14
	1987-88		43	13
Tr	1988-89	Newcastle U	34	4
Tr	1989-90	Leeds U	27	5
Tr	1990-91	Middlesbrough	41	3
	1991-92		38	3
	1992-93		32	9

HILAIRE, Vincent M.

Forest Hill, 10th October 1959

Source	Season	Club	Apps.	Gls
App	1976-77	Crystal Palace	3	-
	1977-78		30	2
	1978-79		31	6
	1979-80		42	5
	1980-81		31	4
	1981-82		36	5
	1982-83		42	5
	1983-84		40	2
Tr	1984-85	Luton T	6	-
Tr	1984-85	Portsmouth	26	7
	1985-86		41	8
	1986-87		41	8
	1987-88		38	2
Tr	1988-89	Leeds U	42	6
	1989-90		2	-
L	1989-90	Stoke C	5	1
Tr	1990-91	Stoke C	10	2
Tr	1991-92	Exeter C	33	4

HIRD, Kevin

Colne, 11th February 1955

Source	Season	Club	Apps.	Gls
App	1973-74	Blackburn R	6	-
	1974-75		2	-
	1975-76		21	6
	1976-77		39	1
	1977-78		42	7
	1978-79		22	6
Tr	1978-79	Leeds U	14	-
	1979-80		39	8
	1980-81		33	4
	1981-82		38	2
	1982-83		39	4
	1983-84		18	1
Tr	1984-85	Burnley	44	16
	1985-86		39	7

HODGE, Stephen B.

Nottingham, 25th October 1962

Source	Season	Club	Apps.	Gls
App	1981-82	Nottingham F	1	-
	1982-83		39	8
	1983-84		39	10
	1984-85		42	12
	1985-86		2	-
Tr	1985-86	Aston Villa	36	8
	1986-87		17	4
Tr	1986-87	Tottenham H	19	4
	1987-88		26	3
Tr	1988-89	Nottingham F	34	7
	1989-90		34	10
	1990-91		14	3
Tr	1991-92	Leeds U	23	7
	1992-93		23	2

HUGHES, Philip A.

Manchester, 19th November 1964

Source	Season	Club	Apps.	Gls
From Apprentice, Manchester United				
	1983-84	Leeds U	2	-
	1984-85		4	-
Tr	1985-86	Bury	41	-
	1986-87		32	-
	1987-88		7	-
Tr	1987-88	Wigan A	31	-
	1988-89		16	-
	1989-90		33	-
	1990-91		19	-
Tr	1991-92	Rochdale	-	-
Tr	1991-92	Scarborough	17	-

IRWIN, Dennis J.

Cork, 31st October 1965

Source	Season	Club	Apps.	Gls
App	1983-84	Leeds U	12	-
	1984-85		41	1
	1985-86		19	-
Tr	1986-87	Oldham A	41	1
	1987-88		43	-
	1988-89		41	2
	1989-90		42	1
Tr	1990-91	Manchester U	34	-
	1991-92		38	4
	1992-93		40	5

JONES, Vincent P. (Vinny)

Watford, 5th January 1965

Source	Season	Club	Apps.	Gls
From Wealdstone				
	1986-87	Wimbledon	22	4
	1987-88		24	2
	1988-89		31	3
Tr	1989-90	Leeds U	45	5
	1990-91		1	-
Tr	1990-91	Sheffield U	31	2
	1991-92		4	-
Tr	1991-92	Chelsea	35	3
	1992-93		7	1

Source	Season	Club	Apps.	Gls
Tr	1992-93	Wimbledon	27	1

KAMARA, Christopher

Middlesbrough, 25th December 1957

Source	Season	Club	Apps.	Gls
App	1975-76	Portsmouth	24	4
	1976-77		39	3
Tr	1977-78	Swindon T	40	10
	1978-79		28	2
	1979-80		34	5
	1980-81		45	4
Tr	1981-82	Portsmouth	11	-
Tr	1981-82	Brentford	31	5
	1982-83		44	11
	1983-84		38	6
	1984-85		39	6
Tr	1985-86	Swindon T	20	1
	1986-87		42	3
	1987-88		25	2
Tr	1988-89	Stoke C	38	4
	1989-90		22	1
Tr	1989-90	Leeds U	11	1
	1990-91		7	-
	1991-92		2	-
Tr	1991-92	Luton T	28	-
	1992-93		21	-
L	1992-93	Sheffield U	8	-
L	1992-93	Middlesbrough	5	-

KELLY, Garry

Drogheda, 9th July 1974

From Home Farm

Source	Season	Club	Apps.	Gls
	1991-92	Leeds U	2	-

KERR, Dylan

Malta, 14th January 1967

From Arcadia Shepherds

Source	Season	Club	Apps.	Gls
	1988-89	Leeds U	3	-
	1989-90		5	-
L	1991-92	Doncaster R	7	1
L	1991-92	Blackpool	12	1
	1992-93	Leeds U	5	-

KERSLAKE, David

London, 19th June 1966

Source	Season	Club	Apps.	Gls
App	1983-84	QPR	-	-
	1984-85		1	-
	1985-86		14	1
	1986-87		3	-
	1987-88		18	5
	1988-89		21	-
	1989-90		1	-
Tr	1989-90	Swindon T	28	-
	1990-91		37	-
	1991-92		39	1
	1992-93		31	-
Tr	1992-93	Leeds U	8	-

LINIGHAN, Andrew

Hartlepool, 18th June 1962

From Smiths B.C.

Source	Season	Club	Apps.	Gls
	1980-81	Hartlepool U	6	-
	1981-82		17	-
	1982-83		45	3
	1983-84		42	1
Tr	1984-85	Leeds U	42	2
	1985-86		24	1
Tr	1985-86	Oldham A	15	1
	1986-87		40	3
	1987-88		32	2
Tr	1987-88	Norwich C	12	2
	1988-89		37	4
	1989-90		37	2
Tr	1990-91	Arsenal	10	-
	1991-92		17	-
	1992-93		21	2

LORIMER, Peter P. K.

Dundee, 14th November 1946

Source	Season	Club	Apps.	Gls
Jnrs	1962-63	Leeds U	1	-
	1964-65		1	-
	1965-66		33	13
	1966-67		30	9
	1967-68		37	17
	1968-69		28	8
	1969-70		39	14
	1970-71		38	12
	1971-72		42	23
	1972-73		41	15
	1973-74		37	12
	1974-75		36	9
	1975-76		29	10
	1976-77		26	3
	1977-78		28	6
	1978-79		3	-
From Toronto				
	1979-80	York C	29	8
From Vancouver				
	1983-84	Leeds U	22	4
	1984-85		40	9
	1985-86		14	4
To Israel				

LUKIC, John

Chesterfield, 11th December 1960

Source	Season	Club	Apps.	Gls
App	1979-80	Leeds U	33	-
	1980-81		42	-
	1981-82		42	-
	1982-83		29	-
Tr	1983-84	Arsenal	4	-
	1984-85		27	-
	1985-86		40	-
	1986-87		36	-
	1987-88		40	-
	1988-89		38	-
	1989-90		38	-
Tr	1990-91	Leeds U	38	-

Source	Season	Club	Apps.	Gls
	1991-92	Leeds U	42	-
	1992-93		39	-

MAGUIRE, Peter J.

Holmfirth, 11th September 1969

YT	1987-88	Leeds U	2	-
Tr	1989-90	Huddersfield T	3	-
	1990-91		4	1
L	1990-91	Stockport Co	2	-

MELROSE, James M.

Glasgow, 7th October 1958

From Eastercraigs

	1975-80	Partick T	122	31
Tr	1980-81	Leicester C	32	9
	1981-82		35	11
	1982-83		5	1
Tr	1982-83	Coventry C	24	8
Tr	1983-84	Glasgow Celtic	29	7
	1984-85		-	-
L	1984-85	Wolverhampton W	7	2
Tr	1984-85	Manchester C	24	7
	1985-86		10	1
Tr	1985-86	Charlton A	11	5
	1986-87		34	14
	1987-88		3	-
Tr	1987-88	Leeds U	4	-
Tr	1987-88	Shrewsbury T	9	1
	1988-89		21	2
	1989-90		19	-

MUMBY, Peter

Bradford, 22nd September 1969

YT	1987-88	Leeds U	5	-
	1988-89		1	-
Tr	1989-90	Burnley	25	4
	1990-91		20	5
	1991-92		1	-

McALLISTER, Gary

Motherwell, 25th December 1964

	1981-86	Motherwell	59	6
Tr	1985-86	Leicester C	31	7
	1986-87		39	10
	1987-88		42	9
	1988-89		46	11
	1989-90		43	10
Tr	1990-91	Leeds U	38	2
	1991-92		42	5
	1992-93		32	5

McCLELLAND, John

Belfast, 7th December 1955

From Portadown

	1974-75	Cardiff C	4	1

From Bangor

Source	Season	Club	Apps.	Gls
	1978-79	Mansfield T	36	1
	1979-80		43	1
	1980-81		46	6
Tr	1981-85	Glasgow Rangers	96	4
Tr	1984-85	Watford	29	1
	1985-86		31	1
	1986-87		41	1
	1987-88		40	-
	1988-89		43	-
Tr	1989-90	Leeds U	3	-
L	1989-90	Watford	1	-
	1990-91	Leeds U	3	-
	1991-92		18	-
L	1991-92	Notts Co	6	-
Tr	1992-93	St. Johnstone	26	-

McCLUSKEY, George

Hamilton, 19th September 1957

	1975-83	Glasgow Celtic	130	54
Tr	1983-84	Leeds U	32	8
	1984-85		19	5
	1985-86		22	3
Tr	1986-89	Hibernian	83	16
Tr	1989-92	Hamilton A	95	34
Tr	1992-93	Kilmarnock	31	11

McDONALD, Robert W.

Aberdeen, 13th April 1955

App	1972-73	Aston Villa	4	-
	1973-74		4	-
	1974-75		18	1
	1975-76		13	2
Tr	1976-77	Coventry C	39	1
	1977-78		42	5
	1978-79		42	4
	1979-80		37	4
	1980-81		1	-
Tr	1980-81	Manchester C	28	4
	1981-82		36	4
	1982-83		32	3
Tr	1983-84	Oxford U	39	4
	1984-85		34	7
	1985-86		14	3
	1986-87		7	-
Tr	1986-87	Leeds U	17	1
	1987-88		1	-
L	1987-88	Wolverhampton W	6	-

McGOLDRICK, John

Coatbridge, 23rd September 1963

From Celtic BC

	1980-83	Glasgow Celtic	-	-
Tr	1983-84	Leeds U	7	-

McGREGOR, John R.

Airdrie, 5th January 1963

From Bargeddie A.

Source	Season	Club	Apps.	Gls
	1979-82	Queen's Park	105	19
Tr	1982-84	Liverpool	-	-
Tr	1983-84	St. Mirren	5	1
Tr	1984-86	Liverpool	-	-
Tr	1985-86	Leeds U	5	-
Tr	1986-87	Liverpool	-	-
Tr	1987-92	Glasgow Rangers	26	-

NEWSOME, Jonathan

Sheffield, 6th September 1970

Source	Season	Club	Apps.	Gls
YT	1989-90	Sheffield W..................	6	-
	1990-91	....	1	-
Tr	1991-92	Leeds U	10	2
	1992-93	....	37	-

NOTEMAN, Kevin S.

Preston, 15th October 1969

Source	Season	Club	Apps.	Gls
YT	1987-88	Leeds U	1	-
Tr	1989-90	Doncaster R..................	30	3
	1990-91	....	42	7
	1991-92	....	34	10
Tr	1991-92	Mansfield T	6	-
	1992-93	....	24	4

O'DONNELL, Christopher

Newcastle, 26th May 1968

Source	Season	Club	Apps.	Gls
App	1986-87	Ipswich T......................	10	-
	1987-88	....	2	-
L	1987-88	Northampton T.............	1	-
	1988-89	Ipswich T......................	2	-
Tr	1989-90	Leeds U	1	-
Tr	1991-92	Exeter C........................	2	-

ORMSBY, Brendan T. C.

Birmingham, 1st October 1960

Source	Season	Club	Apps.	Gls
App	1978-79	Aston Villa	2	-
	1979-80	....	23	-
	1981-82	....	12	-
	1983-84	....	34	2
	1984-85	....	32	2
	1985-86	....	14	-
Tr	1985-86	Leeds U	12	1
	1986-87	....	33	4
	1988-89	....	1	-
L	1989-90	Shrewsbury T	1	-
Tr	1990-91	Doncaster R..................	43	4
	1991-92	....	35	3
Tr	1992-93	Scarborough	16	1

PEARSON, John S.

Sheffield, 1st September 1963

Source	Season	Club	Apps.	Gls
App	1980-81	Sheffield W..................	15	4
	1981-82	....	24	7
	1982-83	....	30	7
	1983-84	....	27	4
	1984-85	....	9	2

Source	Season	Club	Apps.	Gls
Tr	1985-86	Charlton A	42	14
	1986-87	....	19	1
Tr	1986-87	Leeds U	18	4
	1987-88	....	28	6
	1988-89	....	33	1
	1989-90	....	7	-
	1990-91	....	13	1
L	1990-91	Rotherham U	11	5
Tr	1991-92	Barnsley........................	10	1
L	1991-92	Hull C	15	-
	1992-93	Barnsley........................	22	3

PHELAN, Terence M.

Manchester, 16th March 1967

Source	Season	Club	Apps.	Gls
YT	1985-86	Leeds U	14	-
Tr	1986-87	Swansea C	45	-
Tr	1987-88	Wimbledon	30	-
	1988-89	....	29	-
	1989-90	....	34	-
	1990-91	....	29	-
	1991-92	....	37	1
	1992-93	....	-	-
Tr	1992-93	Manchester C...............	37	-

RENNIE, David

Edinburgh, 29th August 1964

Source	Season	Club	Apps.	Gls
App	1983-84	Leicester C...................	15	-
	1984-85	....	3	1
	1985-86	....	3	-
Tr	1985-86	Leeds U	16	2
	1986-87	....	24	-
	1987-88	....	28	2
	1988-89	....	33	1
Tr	1989-90	Bristol C	45	4
	1990-91	....	32	2
	1991-92	....	27	2
Tr	1991-92	Birmingham C.............	17	2
	1992-93	....	18	2
Tr	1992-93	Coventry C	9	-

RITCHIE, Andrew T.

Manchester, 28th November 1960

Source	Season	Club	Apps.	Gls
App	1977-78	Manchester U	4	-
	1978-79	....	17	10
	1979-80	....	8	3
	1980-81	....	4	-
Tr	1980-81	Brighton & HA............	26	5
	1981-82	....	39	13
	1982-83	....	24	5
Tr	1982-83	Leeds U	10	3
	1983-84	....	38	7
	1984-85	....	28	12
	1985-86	....	29	11
	1986-87	....	31	7
Tr	1987-88	Oldham A	36	19
	1988-89	....	31	14
	1989-90	....	38	15
	1990-91	....	31	15
	1991-92	....	14	3

Source	Season	Club	Apps.	Gls
	1992-93	Oldham A	12	3

ROBINSON, Ronald

Sunderland, 22nd October 1966

From S. C. Vaux

Source	Season	Club	Apps.	Gls
	1985-86	Leeds U	16	-
	1986-87		11	-
Tr	1986-87	Doncaster R	12	-
	1987-88		37	1
	1988-89		29	4
Tr	1988-89	West Brom A	1	-
Tr	1989-90	Rotherham U	43	1
	1990-91		38	-
	1991-92		5	1
Tr	1991-92	Peterborough U	27	-
	1992-93		20	-

ROCASTLE, David

Lewisham, 2nd May 1967

Source	Season	Club	Apps.	Gls
App	1984-85	Arsenal	-	-
	1985-86		16	1
	1986-87		36	2
	1987-88		40	7
	1988-89		38	6
	1989-90		33	2
	1990-91		16	2
	1991-92		39	4
Tr	1992-93	Leeds U	18	1

SELLARS, Scott

Sheffield, 27th November 1965

Source	Season	Club	Apps.	Gls
App	1982-83	Leeds U	1	-
	1983-84		19	3
	1984-85		39	7
	1985-86		17	2
Tr	1986-87	Blackburn R	32	4
	1987-88		42	7
	1988-89		46	2
	1989-90		43	14
	1990-91		9	1
	1991-92		30	7
Tr	1992-93	Leeds U	7	-
Tr	1992-93	Newcastle U	13	2

SHARP, Kevin

Canada, 19th September 1974

From Auxerre

Source	Season	Club	Apps.	Gls
	1992-93	Leeds U	4	-

SHERIDAN, John J.

Manchester, 1st October 1964

From Manchester City Juniors

Source	Season	Club	Apps.	Gls
	1982-83	Leeds U	27	2
	1983-84		11	1
	1984-85		42	6
	1985-86		32	4
	1986-87		40	15
	1987-88		38	12
	1988-89		40	7
Tr	1989-90	Nottingham F	-	-
Tr	1989-90	Sheffield W	27	2
	1990-91		46	10
	1991-92		24	6
	1992-93		25	3

SHUTT, Carl S.

Sheffield, 10th October 1961

From Spalding United

Source	Season	Club	Apps.	Gls
	1985-86	Sheffield W	19	9
	1986-87		20	7
	1987-88		1	-
Tr	1987-88	Bristol C	22	9
	1988-89		24	1
Tr	1988-89	Leeds U	3	4
	1989-90		20	2
	1990-91		28	10
	1991-92		14	1
	1992-93		14	-

SIMMONDS, R. Lyndon

Pontypool, 11th November 1966

Source	Season	Club	Apps.	Gls
App	1984-85	Leeds U	1	-
	1985-86		8	3
L	1986-87	Swansea C	8	1
L	1986-87	Rochdale	22	10
Tr	1987-88	Rochdale	43	12

SINCLAIR, Ronald M.

Stirling, 19th November 1964

Source	Season	Club	Apps.	Gls
App	1982-84	Nottingham F	-	-
L	1983-84	Wrexham	11	-
	1984-85	Nottingham F	-	-
L	1984-85	Derby Co	-	-
	1985-86	Nottingham F	-	-
L	1985-86	Sheffield U	-	-
L	1985-86	Leeds U	-	-
Tr	1986-87	Leeds U	8	-
L	1986-87	Halifax T	4	-
	1987-89		-	-
L	1988-89	Halifax T	10	-
Tr	1989-90	Bristol C	27	-
	1990-91		17	-
L	1991-92	Walsall	10	-
Tr	1991-92	Stoke C	26	-
	1992-93		29	-

SNODIN, Ian

Rotherham, 15th August 1963

Source	Season	Club	Apps.	Gls
App	1979-80	Doncaster R	9	1
	1980-81		32	2
	1981-82		33	2
	1982-83		34	3
	1983-84		39	9

Source	Season	Club	Apps.	Gls
	1984-85		41	8
Tr	1985-86	Leeds U	37	5
	1986-87		14	1
Tr	1986-87	Everton	16	-
	1987-88		31	2
	1988-89		23	-
	1989-90		25	-
	1990-91		1	-
	1991-92		-	-

SPEED, Gary A.

Hawarden, 8th September 1969

Source	Season	Club	Apps.	Gls
YT	1988-89	Leeds U	1	-
	1989-90		25	3
	1990-91		38	7
	1991-92		41	7
	1992-93		39	7

STERLAND, Melvyn

Sheffield, 1st October 1961

Source	Season	Club	Apps.	Gls
App	1978-79	Sheffield W	2	1
	1979-80		2	-
	1980-81		22	2
	1981-82		27	-
	1982-83		35	-
	1983-84		39	8
	1984-85		24	2
	1985-86		38	8
	1986-87		30	2
	1987-88		38	8
	1988-89		22	6
Tr	1988-89	Glasgow Rangers	9	3
Tr	1989-90	Leeds U	42	5
	1990-91		38	5
	1991-92		31	6
	1992-93		3	-

STILES, John C.

Manchester, 6th May 1964

From Vancouver Whitecaps

Source	Season	Club	Apps.	Gls
	1984-85	Leeds U	1	-
	1985-86		12	1
	1986-87		29	-
	1987-88		13	1
	1988-89		10	-
Tr	1989-90	Doncaster R	42	2
	1990-91		37	-
	1991-92		10	-
L	1991-92	Rochdale	4	-

STRACHAN, Gordon D.

Edinburgh, 9th February 1957

Source	Season	Club	Apps.	Gls
App	1974-77	Dundee	60	13
Tr	1977-84	Aberdeen	183	70
Tr	1984-85	Manchester U	41	15
	1985-86		28	5
	1986-87		34	4
	1987-88		36	8
	1988-89		21	1
Tr	1988-89	Leeds U	11	3
	1989-90		46	16
	1990-91		34	7
	1991-92		36	4
	1992-93		31	4

STRANDLI, Frank

Norway, 16th May 1972

From IK Start

Source	Season	Club	Apps.	Gls
Tr	1992-93	Leeds U	10	2

SWAN, Peter H.

Leeds, 28th September 1966

Source	Season	Club	Apps.	Gls
YT	1985-86	Leeds U	16	3
	1986-87		7	-
	1987-88		25	8
	1988-89		1	-
Tr	1988-89	Hull C	11	1
	1989-90		31	11
	1990-91		38	12
Tr	1991-92	Port Vale	33	3
	1992-93		38	2

SWINBURNE, Trevor

Houghton-Le-Spring, 20th June 1953

Source	Season	Club	Apps.	Gls
App	1972-73	Sunderland	1	-
	1973-74		1	-
	1974-75		2	-
	1975-76		4	-
	1976-77		2	-
Tr	1977-78	Carlisle U	31	-
	1978-79		45	-
	1979-80		46	-
	1980-81		38	-
	1981-82		46	-
	1982-83		42	-
Tr	1983-84	Brentford	21	-
	1984-85		24	-
Tr	1985-86	Leeds U	2	-
L	1985-86	Doncaster R	4	-
Tr	1985-86	Lincoln C	18	-

TAYLOR, Robert

Horden, 3rd February 1967

From Horden C.W.

Source	Season	Club	Apps.	Gls
	1985-86	Leeds U	2	-
	1986-87		2	-
	1987-88		32	9
	1988-89		6	-
Tr	1988-89	Bristol C	12	8
	1989-90		37	27
	1990-91		39	11

THOMAS, D. Gwyn

Swansea, 26th September 1957

Source	Season	Club	Apps.	Gls
App	1974-75	Leeds U	1	-
	1976-77		7	1
	1977-78		3	1
	1978-79		2	-
	1979-80		3	-
	1980-81		2	-
	1981-82		15	-
	1982-83		39	1
	1983-84		17	-
Tr	1983-84	Barnsley	13	-
	1984-85		40	1
	1985-86		39	5
	1986-87		40	5
	1987-88		42	4
	1988-89		24	2
	1989-90		3	-
Tr	1989-90	Hull C	11	-
	1990-91		11	-
Tr	1991-92	Carlisle U	37	1

THOMAS, Michael R.

Newtown, 7th July 1954

Source	Season	Club	Apps.	Gls
Jnrs	1971-72	Wrexham	20	3
	1972-73		26	-
	1973-74		19	4
	1974-75		31	5
	1975-76		30	2
	1976-77		45	6
	1977-78		43	7
	1978-79		16	6
Tr	1978-79	Manchester U	25	1
	1979-80		35	8
	1980-81		30	2
Tr	1981-82	Everton	10	-
Tr	1981-82	Brighton & HA	20	-
Tr	1982-83	Stoke C	41	11
	1983-84		16	3
Tr	1983-84	Chelsea	17	4
	1984-85		27	5
Tr	1985-86	West Brom A	20	-
L	1985-86	Derby Co	9	-
From Wichita W				
	1988-89	Shrewsbury T	40	1
Tr	1989-90	Leeds U	3	-
L	1989-90	Stoke C	5	-
Tr	1990-91	Stoke C	38	7
Tr	1991-92	Wrexham	26	1
	1992-93		8	1

THOMPSON, Nigel D.

Leeds, 1st March 1967

Source	Season	Club	Apps.	Gls
App	1983-84	Leeds U	1	-
	1985-86		1	-
	1986-87		5	-
L	1987-88	Rochdale	5	-
Tr	1987-88	Chesterfield	4	-
	1988-89		6	-
	1989-90		10	1

TINKLER, Mark

Bishop Auckland, 24th October 1974

Source	Season	Club	Apps.	Gls
YT	1991-92	Leeds U	-	-
	1992-93		7	-

TURNER, Christopher R.

Sheffield, 15th September 1958

Source	Season	Club	Apps.	Gls
App	1976-77	Sheffield W	45	-
	1977-78		23	-
	1978-79		23	-
L	1978-79	Lincoln C	5	-
Tr	1979-80	Sunderland	30	-
	1980-81		27	-
	1981-82		19	-
	1982-83		35	-
	1983-84		42	-
	1984-85		42	-
Tr	1985-86	Manchester U	17	-
	1986-87		23	-
	1987-88		24	-
Tr	1988-89	Sheffield W	29	-
	1989-90		23	-
L	1989-90	Leeds U	2	-
	1990-91	Sheffield W	23	-
Tr	1991-92	Leyton Orient	34	-
	1992-93		17	-

VARADI, Imre

Paddington, 8th July 1959

Source	Season	Club	Apps.	Gls
From Letchworth G.C.				
	1978-79	Sheffield U	10	4
Tr	1979-80	Everton	4	-
	1980-81		22	6
Tr	1981-82	Newcastle U	42	18
	1982-83		39	21
Tr	1983-84	Sheffield W	38	17
	1984-85		38	16
Tr	1985-86	West Brom A	32	9
Tr	1986-87	Manchester C	30	9
	1987-88		32	17
	1988-89		3	-
Tr	1988-89	Sheffield W	20	3
	1989-90		2	-
Tr	1989-90	Leeds U	13	2
	1990-91		6	2
	1991-92		3	-
L	1991-92	Luton T	6	1
	1992-93	Leeds U	4	1
L	1992-93	Oxford U	5	-
Tr	1992-93	Rotherham U	11	4

WALLACE, Ray

Lewisham, 2nd October 1969

Source	Season	Club	Apps.	Gls
YT	1987-88	Southampton	-	-
	1988-89		26	-

Source	Season	Club	Apps.	Gls
	1989-90	Southampton	9	-
	1990-91		-	-
Tr	1991-92	Leeds U	-	-
L	1991-92	Swansea C	2	-
	1992-93	Leeds U	6	-

WALLACE, Rodney S.

Greenwich, 2nd October 1969

Source	Season	Club	Apps.	Gls
YT	1987-88	Southampton	15	1
	1988-89		38	12
	1989-90		38	18
	1990-91		37	14
Tr	1991-92	Leeds U	34	11
	1992-93		32	7

WATSON, Andrew

Aberdeen, 3rd September 1959

From Sunnyside

Source	Season	Club	Apps.	Gls
	1976-83	Aberdeen	97	11
Tr	1983-84	Leeds U	31	7
	1984-85		7	-
Tr	1984-87	Heart of Midlothian	56	6
Tr	1987-89	Hibernian	31	3

WETHERALL, David

Sheffield, 14th March 1971

Source	Season	Club	Apps.	Gls
YT	1989-91	Sheffield W	-	-
Tr	1991-92	Leeds U	1	-
	1992-93		13	1

WHELAN, Noel

Leeds, 30th December 1974

Source	Season	Club	Apps.	Gls
YT	1992-93	Leeds U	1	-

WHITLOW, Michael W.

Northwich, 13th January 1968

From Witton Albion

Source	Season	Club	Apps.	Gls
	1988-89	Leeds U	20	1
	1989-90		29	1
	1990-91		18	1
	1991-92		10	1
Tr	1991-92	Leicester C	5	-
	1992-93		24	1

WHYTE, Christopher A.

Islington, 2nd September 1961

Source	Season	Club	Apps.	Gls
App	1981-82	Arsenal	32	2
	1982-83		36	3
	1983-84		15	2
L	1984-85	Crystal Palace	13	-
	1985-86	Arsenal	7	1

From Los Angeles R.

Source	Season	Club	Apps.	Gls
	1988-89	West Brom A	40	3
	1989-90		44	4
Tr	1990-91	Leeds U	38	3
	1991-92		41	1
	1992-93		34	1

WILLIAMS, Andrew

Birmingham, 29th July, 1962

From Solihull Borough

Source	Season	Club	Apps.	Gls
	1985-86	Coventry C	8	-
	1986-87		1	-
Tr	1986-87	Rotherham U	36	4
	1987-88		36	6
	1988-89		15	3
Tr	1988-89	Leeds U	18	1
	1989-90		16	2
	1990-91		12	-
L	1991-92	Port Vale	5	-
Tr	1991-92	Notts Co	15	1
	1992-93		22	1

WILLIAMS, Gary

Wolverhampton, 17th June 1960

Source	Season	Club	Apps.	Gls
App	1978-79	Aston Villa	23	-
	1979-80		2	-
L	1979-80	Walsall	9	-
	1980-81	Aston Villa	22	-
	1981-82		28	-
	1982-83		36	-
	1983-84		40	-
	1984-85		38	-
	1985-86		25	-
	1986-87		26	-
Tr	1987-88	Leeds U	31	3
	1988-89		8	-
Tr	1989-90	Watford	18	-
	1990-91		24	-
Tr	1991-92	Bradford C	22	-
	1992-93		31	3

WRIGHT, Thomas E.

Dunfermline, 10th January 1966

Source	Season	Club	Apps.	Gls
App	1982-83	Leeds U	4	1
	1983-84		25	8
	1984-85		42	14
	1985-86		10	1
Tr	1986-87	Oldham A	28	7
	1987-88		41	9
	1988-89		43	7
Tr	1989-90	Leicester C	41	3
	1990-91		44	7
	1991-92		44	12
Tr	1992-93	Middlesbrough	36	5

Supporters' Guides : -

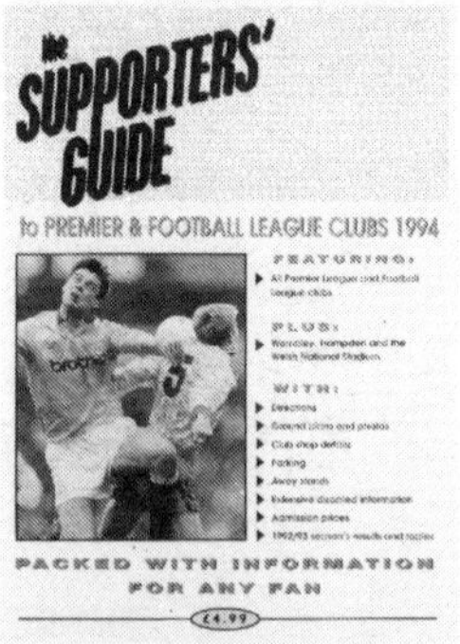

THE SUPPORTERS' GUIDE TO PREMIER & FOOTBALL LEAGUE CLUBS 1994

Featuring :
- all Premier League Clubs
- all Football League clubs
+ 1992/93 season's Results & Tables

120 pages - price £4.99 - post free

THE SUPPORTERS' GUIDE TO NON-LEAGUE FOOTBALL 1994

Featuring :
- all GM/Vauxhall Conference clubs
- all HFS Loans - Premier clubs
- all Beazer Homes - Premier clubs
- all Diadora Premier clubs
+ 180 other major Non-League clubs

112 pages - price £4.99 - post free

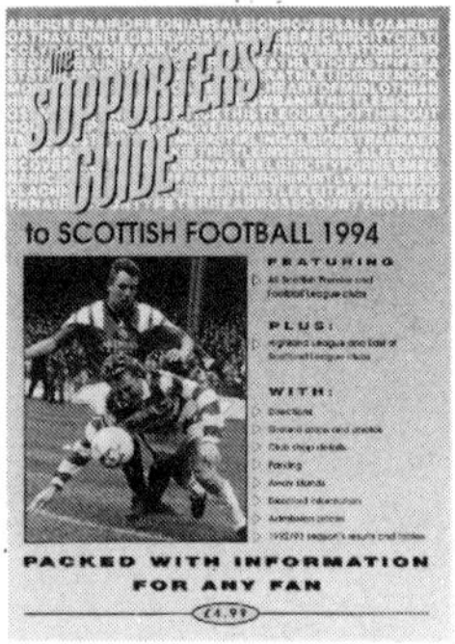

THE SUPPORTERS' GUIDE TO SCOTTISH FOOTBALL 1994

Featuring :
- all Scottish League clubs
- all Highland League clubs
- all East of Scotland League clubs
+ Results, tables

96 pages - price £4.99 - post free

THE SUPPORTERS' GUIDE TO WELSH FOOTBALL 1994

Featuring :
- all Konica League of Wales clubs
- all Cymru Alliance & Abacus League clubs
+ 'The Exiles', Minor League clubs & 1992/93 season's results and tables

96 pages - price £4.99 - post free

order from : -

SOCCER BOOK PUBLISHING LTD.
72 ST. PETERS AVENUE
CLEETHORPES
DN35 8HU
ENGLAND